14, 21, 26, 33 35 46
42

When God Says No

4 10 18 36

4, 10, 18, 36, 46, 49

2 198298

16

Books by Leith Anderson

A Church for the 21st Century
Dying for Change
When God Says No
Winning the Values War in a Changing Culture

9606

LEITH ANDERSON

When God Says No

BETHANY HOUSE PUBLISHERS
MINNEAPOLIS, MINNESOTA 55438

Published by Bethany House Publishers
A Ministry of Bethany Fellowship, Inc.
11300 Hampshire Avenue South
Minneapolis, Minnesota 55438

Printed in the United States of America.

Library of Congress Cataloging-in-Publication Data

Anderson, Leith
    When God says no : finding the God of hope behind the answer we'd
rather not hear / Leith Anderson.
      p.   cm.
    ISBN 1–55661–599–X
      1. Prayer—Christianity. 2. Spiritual life—Christianity.
I. Title.
BV220.A44   1996
248.3'2—dc20   96–10063
                                           CIP

LEITH ANDERSON is the Senior Pastor of Wooddale Church in Eden Prairie, Minnesota. He has degrees from Bradley University, Denver Seminary, and Fuller Theological Seminary. He has written five books and travels extensively speaking to church leadership groups. The Anderson family makes their home in Eden Prairie, Minnesota.

Contents

ONE

The Answer We Don't Want to Hear

I love it when God answers prayer.

Elijah stood on Mount Carmel and prayed for God to win the power struggle against Baal and his arrogant priests. The prophet asked for fire to strike from heaven and inflame wet wood. Fire streaked down and even the water burned away.

A Muslim convert to Christianity received a telephone call in 1990 that his neighborhood was on fire and his house soon would burn. He rushed from his government office to see the flames closing in. There was time to save only his most precious belongings, and when he ran into his house he salvaged a mattress. Standing outside, surrounded by the Muslim neighbors who had persecuted him, he lifted his hands and voice and prayed out loud in the name of Jesus Christ, asking God to intervene and save his home. When he finished with "in Jesus' name. Amen" the thunder boomed, the rains poured and the flames were extinguished.

The neighbors were impressed.

In 1963, a college student was visiting friends in Wisconsin before the start of the summer term at the University of Minnesota. He sensed something was wrong, but didn't know what it was or what to do. He prayed and asked for God's wisdom and direction. He experienced God's answer to abandon his school plans and immediately drive to his parents' home in New Jersey. He drove a thousand miles alone, arriving with little explanation of his behavior. The next day he became seriously ill with measles. Had he gone to Minnesota he would not only have missed school but faced sickness without family or any place to go. The incubation period for the disease dated back to the time of his prayer and God's answer.

One very rainy fall in Colorado, the fields were too muddy for the farmers to harvest the sugar beets. The late date risked total loss of the crop. More rain was forecast. A young pastor visited the farms of his parishioners and prayed for God to intervene and dry the ground. That night the Denver weatherman announced a surprise change in the storm system affecting the area. Instead of rain there would be dry winds. The fields quickly dried and the harvest was completed on time.

A young Minnesota mother with stage three ovarian cancer prayed for healing in 1993. Her advanced disease was being treated with chemotherapy. God said *yes*, moving her dangerous disease into remission.

I believe Elijah's story because I know the Bible is true. I heard the Muslim convert's story firsthand in his native land. I was the college student. I was the pastor in Colorado. The thirty-three-year-old mother is part of the church in Minnesota I have served for twenty years. The list of answers to prayer is long, not just from the Bible and my experiences, but from millions of others around the world and through the centuries.

I love it every time God answers prayer.

But for every story of *answered* prayer there are a thousand stories of *unanswered* prayers—many of them asked by godly saints on their knees pleading with God. God needs no defense. But Christians need an explanation.

Why Does God Say *No* So Often?

Rabbi Harold Kushner wrote *When Bad Things Happen to Good People*[1] after the tragic death of his young son from a frightful disease called "progeria," which makes a child age so rapidly that by grade school his son had shriveled into a little old man. While he was still a boy he died of old age.

Kushner wasn't the first to ask why a good God would allow such a bad thing to happen. He explained that one of three things had to be true about God: either he must not be good, or he must not be strong enough to stop bad things, or he must be unwilling to use his power to remedy our pain. As long as there is pain and suffering in our world, Kushner argued, no one can say that God is altogether good, strong and willing. Kushner concluded that God is good and God is willing, but that he just isn't strong enough to stop all the evil we humans face.

Christians who have wrestled with the claims of Scripture don't resign themselves so easily to the thought of an inferior God. We are convinced from the Bible that God is entirely good, that he can accomplish absolutely anything and that he desires only the best for us—these are foundations for our faith and prayers. Our requests to God are based on assumptions about his character, power and intent. Unanswered prayers, unfortunately, seem to contradict those basic beliefs. Prayer is a simple test of who God is. And God fails the test ten thousand times a day.

In defense of God, Christians have explained that he always answers but that his replies may fit into three different categories: (1) "Yes," (2) "No" or (3) "Later." We have little trouble with "Yes." It's an answer that delights! We quickly and rightly tell as many people as possible that we experienced "a real answer to prayer," although sometimes our celebrations sound as though we take more credit for our praying than we give to God for his answering. Our troubles are with "No" and "Later." Some professed Christians have abandoned their faith because God didn't answer them the way they wanted or expected.

Those who are so gravely disappointed with God usually aren't evil people. They are mothers and fathers who sincerely believed God could and would heal their children from terminal diseases. They are missionaries praying for success in evangelizing the peoples to whom God has called them. They are children who kneel beside their beds at night and ask God to give Daddy a new job or to stop him from hurting Mommy. They are police officers who pray for protection, students who ask for help in their exams, relief workers who plead for food to feed starving families and government leaders who seek divine wisdom in controversial legislative votes. They are good, well-intentioned people, and we would be hard pressed to label their prayers as anything but good and reasonable. We see no clear-cut reasons why God would turn them down.

It isn't easy to keep believing in a God who refuses to heal a sick baby or who rejects a thousand sincere prayers.

Kim weighed just four pounds when she was born in Korea and abandoned by her mother. By the time her American family adopted her she had been diagnosed with syphilis, hepatitis, ear infections and pneumonia. As a nine-month-old she couldn't crawl, grasp a toy or display emotion. At first she thrived on her new family's love. But by the time she started preschool the teachers and family knew something more was wrong. Kim had Attention Deficit Disorder (ADD), learning disabilities, asthma and Tourette's syndrome.

Her aunt prayed and prayed for a miracle that would allow her to be a normal child, or at least be free from the great personal and social problems of Tourette's, a neurological disorder that causes involuntary body movements and vocal outbursts. She has in full sincerity offered her life to God if he would just spare her niece the emotional pain and agony she will surely endure. "God appears to be ignoring my fervent requests," she says. "This is severely trying my faith, that he would allow an innocent child to suffer most of her life. Whom has she hurt?

What has she done to deserve this? I pray he isn't using her life to teach others a lesson. She isn't getting better. I do continue to pray. But for how long? I'm losing hope. Did God send her to us so she could have opportunities she would never have had in Korea? Is that the best I can expect? It breaks my heart to see her struggle, knowing the prognosis is more suffering and hurt and emotional pain. I'm fighting to keep my faith, knowing that God doesn't seem to care. I can't perform a miracle for her, but God can. She is so innocent and undeserving of this. Why won't God spare her when he has the power? He has answered my prayers before. I'd give all those answers back, except for maybe one, if he would grant my prayers for my niece. It would be so easy for him."

I admit that I have shared the doubts and struggle of unanswered prayers—not to the point of joining the ranks of those who abandon God, but certainly to the point of telling God my deep frustration with him. Almost every day for more than twenty years I have prayed the same specific prayer: that God would accomplish his great good in the life of a particular loved one. I have worded that prayer in as many combinations as my vocabulary and imagination can create. I have quoted the Bible to God, hoping that using his own words might work better than my inventions. I have asked him to be blunt with me, to tell me to quit asking because the whole prayer routine is useless. I have even explained to God the obvious benefits of doing what I request, coming close to talking down to the Almighty—as if he could get it better when I put it into words he could understand. So far the answer is still *no*.

There is some comfort in knowing I'm not alone. Actually, the company of the denied is rather impressive.

No to a Sufferer Named Job

Personal pain motivates prayer like little else. Even the unbelieving scream for God's relief if life hurts enough. Nothing is unusual or inappropriate, certainly, about a good person asking for God's help.

Job was one of the best of men. He deserves to be remembered in the Bible for his godliness, character, success and fame. It is ironic that he is instead known best for his pain.

His hurt began with simultaneous tragedies that took the lives of all ten of his children on the same day. He suffered an unspeakable hollowness of heart at the graves of the sons and daughters whom he loved, children for whom he had frequently prayed.

As if that weren't enough he soon went from prosperity to poverty and health to sickness. Job never prayed for his children to come back to life. He never asked for his lost wealth to suddenly reappear. But he did ask God for relief from chronic pain and debilitating disease.

I remember the first two times I witnessed men in terrible pain. The first was when I was a teenager. I was driving along a divided highway when an accident occurred on the opposite side of the road. I saw a car careen out of control into a gas station, knocking out the pumps and crashing into the station office. It was a fiery mess. I quickly drove off the highway and into the station parking lot. I heard the anguished screams of the gas station attendant, who was pinned against the station wall by a car erupting in flames. He cried for help that I couldn't give.

The second time was at a Denver hospital, making my first hospital call as a student studying for the ministry. I didn't know the man I went to see, a terminal patient on the cancer ward, and was glad that I was only an observer accompanying a more seasoned pastor. The man in the bed pleaded with a nurse to give him an injection to lessen his pain. She said that the doctor's orders didn't allow another shot for two more hours. Knowing there was nothing I could say to help this man in his agony, I left the room and walked down the hallway alone—trembling and sick to my stomach.

Uncontrolled pain is a horrible thing to see and even worse

to suffer. At both the gas station and the hospital I was helpless. Yet I know beyond any doubt I would have helped if I could. If it had been within my power I would have lifted the car and pulled the station attendant to safety. If I were a doctor at liberty to administer morphine I would have given an injection in an instant, without hesitation. I still wonder at the senseless logic of withholding relief from a miserable dying man.

God can always help. He who has the power to move mountains certainly is capable of sliding a crashed car back a few feet. He who created human anatomy could convince a physician or nurse to spare a few milligrams of morphine. He who loved Job and counted him as the best example of faithfulness on earth certainly could have answered that tormented man's prayer. Job said, "I cry out to you, O God, but you do not answer; I stand up, but you merely look at me" (Job 30:20). The man whose name has become a synonym for patience spoke words that touch my heart thousands of years later:

> When I hoped for good, evil came;
> when I looked for light, then came darkness.
> The churning inside me never stops;
> days of suffering confront me.
> I go about blackened, but not by the sun;
> I stand up in the assembly and cry for help.
> I have become a brother of jackals,
> a companion of owls.
> My skin grows black and peels;
> my body burns with fever.
> My harp is tuned to mourning,
> and my flute to the sound of wailing.
>
> Job 30:26–31

Had Job asked me for help I would have helped him in any way I could. Job asked God for help. God could have helped him in countless ways. God said *no.*

Job's story has been reread by millions of sufferers since. What is surprising is that so many have found comfort in a biography that recounts God's repeated silence to pain. Maybe sufferers supernaturally know something that doesn't make sense to the rest of us. It would seem that if God won't do what is asked by a deserving man like Job, there isn't much hope that God will help any of us lesser sufferers.

No to a Dad Named David

Considering that the Bible describes David as "a man after [God's] own heart" (Acts 13:22), you would expect his prayers to get preferential treatment. After all, he was an ancestor of Jesus, God's chosen king of Israel and the author of most of the Psalms.

One of David's darkest moments came with the illness of his newborn son. David's boy was conceived in hot and sinful passion with his next-door neighbor's wife. But that shouldn't be a reason for God to let the baby die; the child, after all, didn't choose his parents or the circumstances of his conception. Yet the prophet Nathan, after confronting David's adultery and hearing his repentance, told David that "The LORD has taken away your sin. You are not going to die. But because by doing this you have made the enemies of the LORD show utter contempt, the son born to you will die" (2 Samuel 12:13–14). It was shortly after that prophecy that the baby became deathly sick.

The fact that the baby's father was a king made no difference. Even royal children die. But David was a man of God, a veteran of faith, an experienced person of prayer. He knew what to do. He did it with zeal, fasting and praying for seven days, begging God to save his boy's life. So intense were the king's prayers that he refused to go to bed at night. He just lay on the ground and prayed and prayed. His servants feared he would die even if his child didn't.

The exact words of David's prayers aren't recorded, but they aren't hard to figure out. They must have been like the prayers of other desperate parents pleading for the life of a be-loved child. David reasoned with God that the punishment should come to him, not his son. He no doubt offered his own life in exchange for his son's. He asked God what it was he wanted. He asked God what great feat he could do for God. He repeated the same prayers again and again, wondering if his wording or inflection or intensity made any difference. Those who observed him thought he would kill himself if the baby died.

As the father of four children, I have prayed like that. Once it was in the hospital when our young son stopped breathing and the staff sounded the emergency and leaped to save his life. My heart pounded. My prayers were panicky. *Pleading.* I've lost track of the times when Charleen and I took turns pacing the floor with a listless toddler aflame with fever, wondering why the doctor took so long to call back. We both prayed as we paced the floor, worrying about the brain damage the fever might be causing. On other late nights I prayed for teenage children not yet home, fearing the worst and praying for the best.

I don't know David's exact words to God, but I have an idea how he felt. He shared the feelings of most parents, the prayers of every mother and father whose deep love compels them to pray hard.

King David's awful situation was far from unique. In a sur-vey of those who felt God had let their prayers go unanswered the greatest response came from parents who agonized over their children. Their stories are the most passionate and pain-ful, usually focusing on the diseases and deaths of young chil-dren or the misbehavior of older children.

After David and Anne Hann suffered two miscarriages in 1991, they prayed fervently for a full-term pregnancy and a healthy baby. As time passed and Anne couldn't become preg-nant they began to assume God's answer was *no*. Disappoint-ment turned to delight, though, when Anne became pregnant in 1993 and they had a son on January 27, 1994. Matthew

Charles Hann appeared to be perfect. The Hanns went home with thanksgiving in their hearts. But Matthew's color turned bluish when he was just ten days old. The Hanns took him to the doctor at 2:00 P.M. and to a children's hospital by 5:00 P.M. He was diagnosed with a heart defect unlike any the physicians had seen before. The decision on appropriate medical treatment was difficult, but open heart surgery seemed the best choice.

Anne and David prayed for their son to be healed. God said *no*. Matthew died during surgery on February 15, 1994, just nineteen days old. Matthew's parents have had great difficulty understanding why he died. They have grieved. They have sensed God's healing in their lives, believing that Matthew's life had a purpose and that it was fulfilled in his short lifespan. Yet they admit they cannot fathom that purpose just yet. They live knowing they will probably wrestle to find a reason for their family's tragedy until they are reunited with Matthew in heaven. "God is good," Anne says, "and as a family we have grown tremendously in our faith."

The baby son of David, the man after God's own heart, also died. God said *no*.

As a pastor I have stood near as parents have heard God say *no*. The silence of heaven can be deafening. The death of a child is more awful than any description could ever tell, an unfathomable combination of lost life, unfulfilled dreams and painful heartbreak, wrapped in a profound sense that the essential order of the generations has been broken (children are meant to bury their parents, not the other way around). I have cried with parents who struggled to find explanations not of a child's death but of disabilities and dysfunctions. They blame themselves if the malfunction is genetic, as if they could control the unannounced behavior of their genes. They blame themselves if "something else could have been done," playing the "what if" script a thousand times over.

Parents blame themselves when the product of the best of dreams in the best of homes ends up in juvenile court, a prodigal child. They blame themselves for the bad choices of adult children, as if their parental influence were responsible for everything their offspring would ever do. I have gently reminded them that even the Perfect Father had children who sinned and died. Not even the best of parents are guaranteed perfect results. Sometimes they seem comforted by words. Often they pass them off as theological jargon impotent against life's harshest pains.

Eventually those who have prayed ask why God didn't keep tragedy at bay: Why didn't God stop this horror from striking? Why didn't God save my son? What kind of God allows an innocent child to suffer such deformity or writhe in so much pain? Where was God when our children were deciding between good and evil—couldn't he have nudged them in the other direction? While it is true that they sincerely prayed, "God, I know this is up to you; I know it is your will, not mine, that counts; I trust you to choose," they never really expected the answer God gave.

When we pray like David for our children, we never want to hear God say *no*.

No to a Saint Named Paul

Paul began as a skeptic—worse yet, a persecutor—of Christianity. He was a hard man to convert. But when he finally believed, his zeal was converted along with his soul. He trekked and sailed and evangelized from Jerusalem to Rome. The churches he started became the backbone of first-century Christendom. He wrote thirteen of the twenty-seven books of the New Testament and much of the book of Acts is about him, even though it was authored by Luke. Other than Jesus, Paul is the most prominent character in the New Testament. And other than Jesus, Paul tells us more about prayer than anyone else. Prayers pepper his writings.

When we eavesdrop on Paul's conversations with God we

can't help but conclude that he really knew how to pray:

> For this reason I kneel before the Father, from whom his whole family in heaven and on earth derives its name. I pray that out of his glorious riches he may strengthen you with power through his Spirit in your inner being, so that Christ may dwell in your hearts through faith. And I pray that you, being rooted and established in love, may have power, together with all the saints, to grasp how wide and long and high and deep is the love of Christ, and to know this love that surpasses knowledge—that you may be filled to the measure of all the fullness of God.
>
> Now to him who is able to do immeasurably more than all we ask or imagine, according to his power that is at work within us, to him be glory in the church and in Christ Jesus throughout all generations, for ever and ever! Amen.
>
> Ephesians 3:14–21

Not only were Paul's prayers eloquent, they were also effective. At least a partial answer to this prayer of Paul is given in Jesus' report card on the Ephesians: "I know your deeds, your hard work and your perseverance. I know that you cannot tolerate wicked men, that you have tested those who claim to be apostles but are not, and have found them false. You have persevered and have endured hardships for my name, and have not grown weary" (Revelation 2:2–3).

No doubt about it: Paul was well connected to God and God's power. He reports that he was able to perform "signs, wonders and miracles" (2 Corinthians 12:12). Depending on how we understand 2 Corinthians 12:1–4, Paul may have even died and gone to heaven and come back to life again. Or he may at least have visited heaven for a brief preview and lived to tell about it.

You would think that someone so close to God, so experienced in prayer, and so effective with supernatural power would get a *yes* from God when asking for a small personal favor. Not necessarily! In that same chapter of 2 Corinthians Paul reports a definite *no*:

> To keep me from becoming conceited because of these surpassingly great revelations, there was given to me a thorn in the flesh, a messenger of Satan, to torment me. Three times I pleaded with the LORD to take it away from me. But he said to me, "My grace is sufficient for you, for my power is made perfect in weakness."
>
> 2 Corinthians 12:7–9

Paul left twenty centuries of Bible readers guessing about what was bothering him. Some say it was malaria, a disease that comes and goes; this would explain why he prayed for healing on three different occasions. Others think he suffered from poor eyesight and wanted God to give him normal vision; this guess fits well with mentions of his "illness" and the willingness of his friends to "tear out their eyes and give them to him" (Galatians 4:13–15), plus his personal tag at the end of Galatians: "See what large letters I use as I write to you with my own hand!" (6:11).

Whatever Paul's malady, he prayed passionately to be healed:

"thorn in my flesh" sounds painful

"messenger from Satan" sounds evil

"tormented" sounds chronic

"three times" sounds frequent

"pleaded with the Lord" sounds desperate.

Three times God said *no*.

If Paul had power from God to heal others, why couldn't he heal himself? If God's approval was on Paul's life and work, why didn't God help him out? The same questions have been asked by missionaries who have been called by God, learned a language and then seen foreign governments deny their visas in spite of repeated prayers. The same quandary is faced by modern saints who successfully pray for friends and strangers to be healed but can't get God to say anything but *no* to their personal pleas for comparatively small miracles. Paul must have bordered on embarrassment that he could survive a deadly snakebite and then heal just about every sick person on the island of Malta with simple prayers (Acts 28:1–9), but he couldn't get God to fix his eyes.

God doesn't act the way we choose. He doesn't always give the answer we want. *No* is a common word in the divine vocabulary with regard to prayer—even when answering the greatest of the saints.

Painful Prayers

There is truth in the unanswered prayers of Job, David and Paul, but there may not be comfort. It hurts to hear *no*—especially when the prayers we pray deal with the deepest and most important issues of our lives: chronic pain, vital relationships, powerful emotions, life and death, eternal destiny. These aren't frivolous requests, selfish whims. When our prayers reflect what we believe God wants, we can't understand how God could deny his own desires.

How do we rise above the pain and come to believe God is right and good even when he says *no* to our most pained prayers? How do we still believe? How do we understand? And, most important of all, how do we go on when all hope is gone and the divine *no* is final?

These are more than academic questions to be argued in a classroom. They are questions of the heart. These are the great questions of life and faith. The answers are not short, simple or easy.

Sonia Miller is a college student who was eighteen years old when her grandmother was diagnosed with cancer of the lungs, liver and spine. Her whole family joined in prayer for healing. Sonia says that "it was difficult to watch her struggle for breath and to see her in so much pain." They continued to pray but the pain continued. Although expected to live at least five months, Sonia's grandmother died in two months. God's answer was *no*. "God had not forgotten us," Sonia now explains. "He was with us all along. We have seen God move in different ways in our family. Although it was difficult, I knew that God was with me and was going to work all things out for his glory, which he did."

There *are* answers that allow us to go on when all hope is gone, when God's *no* is settled and unchangeable. The answers are found in the Bible, in the experiences of others, and especially in a personal relationship with God. Some answers are obvious, others never quite perfectly satisfying. Some are answers for the head; most are answers for the heart. Jesus invites us to explore these answers: Jesus said, "Ask and it will be given to you; seek and you will find; knock and the door will be opened to you" (Matthew 7:7).

Asking God "Why?"

God, I don't ever want to hear you say no. I wouldn't ask if I didn't really want a yes.

If you will not say yes, will you at least tell me why you say no? Help me to understand your ways and wisdom. Show me in simple human terms the complexity of your decisions.

For my part, I will begin to trust you always to be right even when I can't understand. I will try not to pry for answers you want to keep secret. I admit that I have no right to demand information you choose not to give.

It isn't that I must have specific explanations for every prayer you refuse, but help me to understand you enough to list correctly your range of reasons and to believe that there is always a valid divine explanation for every no, even though I may never be told. Amen.

Notes

1. Harold S. Kushner, *When Bad Things Happen to Good People* (New York: Schocker, 1981).

Two

Can Prayer Ever Be Bad for Us?

Aurelius Augustinus was born in A.D. 354 in Tagaste, a city of North Africa near the modern city of Qacentina (Constantine), Algeria. The most passionate prayer of his godly Christian mother was painfully answered *no*.

Augustine, as he is better known to us, was the son of a religiously mixed marriage. His father followed pagan Roman religion, with its heathen idols and temples that indulged human passions with sexual excess. As a member of the city council, his father was a prominent member of the community who provided his son with an education in Greek and Roman philosophy—then considered the only path to truth, happiness and success. Young Augustine, deeply influenced by his father and his heritage, became a brilliant philosopher, orator and teacher. He also became sexually promiscuous, a seeker of constant pleasure—what today we might call a rich, educated playboy.

His mother was his father's complete opposite. Monica was

a committed and devout Christian. Her peace and purpose attracted her son, but not enough for him to follow her faith. His beliefs and behavior broke his mother's heart. While she prayed often for her son's salvation, her prayers were never more fervent than when Augustine decided to leave North Africa to sail for Rome. To her adult son it was the opportunity of his lifetime. Rome offered the best of philosophers and the greatest of sensual pleasures. There he could expand his thinking, exercise his gifts and indulge his pleasures. Though his mother begged him not to go, he booked passage and prepared to leave.

Monica could imagine nothing worse than losing her son to the evil capital of the empire. She feared she would never see him again. Far worse, she feared he would be eternally lost. She prayed to God. She pleaded with Augustine.

She wouldn't give up. At the harbor she prayed and wept, yearning for God to intervene and stop her son from leaving. Her passionate prayers and flowing tears became legendary. Centuries later Spanish pioneers stood on the coast of southern California and watched the sun's rays sparkle on the Pacific Ocean. They said the sparkles looked like Monica's tears and named the place Santa Monica in her memory.

It must have been hard to comprehend God's *no*. If ever there were a woman I would expect God to hear, it was Monica. If ever there were a prayer God should answer, it would be for a prodigal son to be spared from greater sin. With her tears flowing and heart breaking she watched the ship sail north, her beloved, rebellious son aboard. She must have been tempted to think God cruel.

The truth behind the seeming cruelty was that God loved Augustine too much to give what his mother asked.

Augustine's dreams and Monica's nightmares all came true. He chased after a string of non-Christian movements and ancient philosophies. He indulged himself in sin. He fathered a child by a woman he lived with but never married. Augustine became professionally successful, moving to Milan and teaching philosophy and rhetoric to the sons of the wealthy and powerful.

Augustine turned against God, but God did not turn against Augustine. While teaching his students Augustine came to the private conclusion that the philosophies he taught were untrue. He was entrapped in an immoral lifestyle, yet wishing he could find freedom and morality.

On a hot August afternoon in A.D. 386, God forever changed this thirty-two-year-old teacher. He describes what happened in his autobiographical *Confessions:*

> I was unwilling to enter His narrow way. And it was becoming a heavy grief to me that I continued to act like a worldling, now that I longed for the sweetness and beauty of your eternal home. The reason for my unwillingness was that I was bound by my love for women.
>
> Oh yes, I was certain that it was better to commit myself to your love than to give in to my sensuality. Still I kept giving the slow, sleepy reply: "Soon, Lord. I will come to you soon."
>
> But "soon" had no ending. Because I was so violently held by my evil habit, my mind was being torn. I wanted freedom, but I was being held as if against my will—and I suppose I contributed to this state of confusion, since I willingly allowed myself to slide into sin.
>
> But you, O Lord, used the changed lives of other men and women like a mirror to keep turning me around to face myself. You set me in front of my own face so that I might see how deformed, how crooked and sordid and stained and ulcerous I was. Horrified, I turned and tried to run from myself—only to find that you were there, too, thrusting me in front of myself. You wanted me to discover my iniquity and hate it, because it bound me and kept me from going with you.
>
> Yet my soul hung back.
>
> So I lived for a long while in a silent, trembling misery, for I was afraid of giving up my sin as much as I feared

death—even though it was because of my evil I was wasting away to death!

Then one day, as I was reading the epistles of Paul, a great storm of agitation began to billow within my soul. My heart and mind and even my face became wild, as this inner storm built. There was a garden attached to our house, and I rushed out there so that no one would see me in such a wild state.

And there I was, going mad on my way to sanity— dying on my way to life!

My mind grew frantic: I boiled with anger at myself for not giving myself over to your law that brings Life. All my bones cried out that if I surrendered fully to you I would find myself free and singing your praises to the skies. I knew that it took but one step—a distance not as far as I had run from my own house to this bench where I had collapsed in my grief. To go over to your side, to arrive fully on your side, required nothing other than the will to go—but to will strongly and totally, not to turn and twist a half-wounded will so that one part of me would keep rising up and struggling, while the other part kept me bound to earth.

This inability to decide—for God or for my Self—was torturing me. I pulled at my hair, beat my forehead, locked my fingers together, gripped my knees with both hands. My whole body felt the agony of my desire to go over to you, but I could not will my soul to rise and cross over to God. I knew that what held me was such a small thing, and yet I turned and twisted as one held on to a chain, as if my own agonizing might finally break it somehow.

Inwardly, I cried, "Let it be done now. *Now!*"

And you, O Lord, were standing in the secret places of my soul all along! With your severe mercy, you redoubled the lashes of fear and shame, so that I would not give up again, which would mean that chain which bound me from you would bind me more strongly than ever before.

I kept imagining the voices of mistresses, as they

plucked at my garment of flesh, whispering, "Can you really send us away? How can you live without us?"

I ran further from the house, into the garden, and flung myself down on the ground under a fig tree. Tears streamed and flooded from my eyes. I cried out, "How long will I keep saying, 'soon' and 'tomorrow'? Why can't I put an end to my uncleanness this very minute?"

And at that very moment I heard from a neighboring house a child's voice—whether a boy or a girl I couldn't tell—singing over and over: "Take and read, take and read. . . ." It was like the song in a child's game, but I'd never heard it before.

These words came into my heart with the force of a divine command: "Take and read. . . ."

I forced myself to stop crying and got up off the ground. I went back into the garden to the place where I had left the Scriptures, which I had carried outside with me—for I believed I had heard nothing less than a divine command to open the book and read the first passage I found.

I snatched the book, opened it and read the first passage my eye fell upon: "Let us behave decently . . . not in orgies and drunkenness, not in sexual immorality and debauchery. . . . Rather, clothe yourselves with the Lord Jesus Christ, and do not think about how to gratify the desires of the sinful nature" (Romans 13:13–14).

I did not need to read further. There was no need to. For as soon as I reached the end of the sentence, it was as though my heart was filled with light and with confidence. All the shadows of my doubt were swept away.[1]

It was a good thing God didn't grant Monica's request to keep her son in Tagaste. It was in his leaving that he finally came home to God. The Lord heard his mother's pleas and saw her tears. But God knew that Augustine first needed to expand his world, explore other philosophies and indulge his desires before he would weary of sin and self and open his life to Jesus Christ. There were other Christians who needed to influence her son; Monica was not enough. God had men and women in Italy who would become the mirrors Augustine needed to face himself and his sin. God foresaw a garden in Milan and a child's simple song on an August afternoon. God was so bent on the best interests of Monica and Augustine that he had to say *no* to a mother's prayers.

The rest of the story is far-reaching. In A.D. 387 Augustine was baptized by Saint Ambrose, the bishop of Milan, who had great influence on Augustine's thinking and faith. The teacher from Tagaste not only became a Christian, but grew into a powerful preacher, a bishop of the church and one of the most influential Christian theologians of history. He defended orthodoxy against assaults of heresy. He intervened to stop a looming new wave of persecution. His writings powerfully influenced later Christian leaders and theologians such as John Calvin and Martin Luther. His thought impacted the philosophies of Immanuel Kant and Blaise Pascal. He even has a city of northeastern Florida named in his memory, St. Augustine.

It isn't that God ignored Monica's prayers. More than Monica knew, God knew what she wanted. Even more than Monica the mother, God the Father wanted the best for Augustine. God answered her prayers, though not quite the way she asked or expected.

God graciously declined her request in order to give her something better.

When we ask for something from God we assume we ask for what is best for us. Only the most perverted of prayers knowingly asks God for evil. The problem is this: we don't always know what is best. Often that becomes apparent to us long after we have asked—and been denied.

Mindi Jennings is a twenty-one-year-old customer service representative who became infatuated with a college student when she was a junior in high school. From the moment her older sister introduced her to him she dreamed of marrying him. When he called her the night of her junior prom she was filled with so much happiness she couldn't concentrate on her date for the evening. That was only the beginning. Mindi says that "I went to visit my sister at college and spent more time with him than I did with her. I was in heaven! By the time I had to leave, we decided to be more than friends. We kept in contact, fell in love, he even came to see me. I thought everything was going great. My parents were in support of it and everyone thought he was a great guy. We knew we were going to get married. I even believed this was God's will."

When the dream began to unravel Mindi became bitter against her friends, family and God. "How could God give him to me and then take him away?" she asked. "God knew how much I wanted to be with him. How could he, out of nowhere, say *no*?"

Mindi learned a lesson God has taught millions of times: what we want from God isn't what is best for us. God has something better that we cannot imagine—or manage to pray—at the time. "Through the biggest trial of my life," Mindi adds, "I came to realize that when I finally gave up, surrendered and obeyed, God's saying *no* turned into God's saying *yes*. Two months later I met the husband God had saved for me. And I am thankful to God more than anyone will ever know that he did say *no*."

No can be one of God's best gifts to us!

When God Says *Yes* to Less Than Best

It would be comforting to imagine that God always protects us from lesser things and brings us better things. Prayer and God aren't that simple. God has a range of responses to our requests. And we can find clear examples from the Bible that God sometimes lets us have what we want, saying *yes* to less-than-best requests.

The people of Israel demanded a king. That wasn't what God had in mind. He intended to be the king of Israel himself, to establish a theocracy rather than a monarchy. God wanted Israel to be utterly different from the heathen nations surrounding them. To have no king was visible evidence of that difference. But the people didn't want to be different. They wanted a king just like the other nations: "Give us a king to lead us" (1 Samuel 8:6).

Perhaps fearing God's displeasure the people asked the prophet Samuel to pray their wishes for them and make their demands known to God. Samuel didn't like the idea. But it was his job to speak to the people for God and speak to God for the people. He relayed the request, knowing it was the wrong thing to pray. Samuel was smarter than the rest of his nation and he felt bad for what he asked of God. God assured him that he shouldn't take the people's anger personally: "It is not you they have rejected, but they have rejected me as their king" (1 Samuel 8:7).

Before granting their request God told Samuel to warn Israel of the consequences of their demand. Samuel bluntly predicted that a king would draft their sons into the army, force their daughters into the labor force, tax their produce and possessions, confiscate their best land and make everyone worse off than they were before. "When that day comes, you will cry out for relief from the king you have chosen, and the LORD will not answer you in that day" (1 Samuel 8:18).

Then, fully knowing it was less than best, God gave Israel the king they prayed for. And he gave them a pretty good king at that. Saul was tall and handsome and popular and the people cheered with delight. At first Saul was a humble man surprised by his selection. Yet what started with promise ended in disaster. The new king's ego grew even larger than his crown and throne. Initial successes crumbled into royal selfishness and cowardice. Worst of all, the king who was to be God's regent on earth became hopelessly alienated from the Lord whose people he ruled. The nation collapsed into disarray and civil war.

They would all have been better off if God had said *no* in the first place.

Hezekiah was a much later, much better king of Israel—one of the best. "Hezekiah trusted in the LORD, the God of Israel. There was no one like him among all the kings of Judah, either before him or after him. He held fast to the LORD and did not cease to follow him; he kept the commands the LORD had given Moses. And the LORD was with him; he was successful in whatever he undertook" (2 Kings 18:5–7).

He was a good man and a good king. Hezekiah was especially effective in prayer. At one point the seemingly invincible armies of Assyria were positioned to defeat Israel. Everyone panicked when the enemy general Sennacherib sent a threatening letter to Hezekiah and the nation of Israel. But Hezekiah was a godly man who knew what to do in a crisis. He laid the letter before God and uttered one of the most eloquent and effective prayers recorded in the Bible:

> "O LORD, God of Israel, enthroned between the cherubim, you alone are God over all the kingdoms of the earth. You have made heaven and earth. Give ear, O LORD, and hear; open your eyes, O LORD, and see; listen to the words Sennacherib has sent to insult the living God.
>
> "It is true, O LORD, that the Assyrian kings have laid waste these nations and their lands. They have thrown their gods into the fire and destroyed them, for they were not gods but only wood and stone, fashioned by men's hands. Now, O LORD our God, deliver us from his hand, so that all kingdoms on earth may know that you alone, O LORD, are God."
>
> 2 Kings 19:15–19

God answered big, sending his angel during the night to kill 185,000 Assyrian soldiers. Sennacherib, his army decimated, retreated to his capital in Nineveh, where he was assassinated by his own sons. This was one of history's most spectacular answers to prayer!

Next came Hezekiah's personal crisis. The king became desperately ill. Lest Hezekiah entertain any doubt that he was near death, the prophet Isaiah warned him that "This is what the LORD says: Put your house in order, because you are going to die; you will not recover" (2 Kings 20:1).

Even a king quakes when he looks death in the eye. The exhilaration of yesterday's military victory isn't enough to keep personal emotions rallied against an imminent end to life. Hezekiah did exactly what most of us would do. He asked for a miracle. He prayed for time—an extension to his life. It was consistent with the way he had handled crises before. If asking God for the impossible had worked for the nation, why shouldn't it work for the king? When Hezekiah heard his dismal prognosis, he turned his head to the wall and prayed with bitter tears: "Remember, O LORD, how I have walked before you faithfully and with wholehearted devotion and have done what is good in your eyes" (2 Kings 20:3).

You and I have something in common with King Hezekiah. We love life. We dread death. Nothing wrong with that. God made us that way. I am convinced Hezekiah's prayer would have better been denied. I would have hoped Hezekiah would submit to what God said was to happen and face his death courageously. But I wasn't the one lying on the royal deathbed. If I were told today that I will die tomorrow I would pray as persuasively as I could. I would beg God for longer life. When we face death there is only one logical request, only one desirable answer to our prayers. We want God to grant healing and life. Anything else seems cruel and unloving. It is unimaginable that death could be our best alternative.

God said *yes*. He answered another of Hezekiah's prayers with a miracle: "I have heard your prayer and seen your tears; I will heal you. On the third day from now you will go up to the temple of the LORD. I will add fifteen years to your life" (2 Kings 20:5–6).

Two important events marked the following fifteen years that seemed neither particularly unusual nor memorable at the time. The first was the arrival of a delegation of visitors from the prince of the neighbor nation Babylon. They brought get-well greetings and gifts. Celebrating his new health and delighted to have company, Hezekiah took his guests on a comprehensive tour of the palace. He showed them everything, including all the valuable treasures of Israel—silver, gold, spices and fine oil. The second important event was the birth of Hezekiah's son Manasseh three years after Hezekiah's healing. When King Hezekiah's fifteen years were finally up he was succeeded by King Manasseh, who was only twelve years old at the time but who reigned for the next fifty-five years.

These two seemingly insignificant events drastically reshaped Israel's future. The get-well visitors turned out to be spies who reported the wealth and set in motion events that eventually led Babylon to conquer Israel and carry the people away into slavery. And in the meantime King Manasseh took the nation from the heights of his godly father's reign into a spiritual freefall. Manasseh "did evil in the eyes of the LORD, following the detestable practices of the nations the LORD had driven out before the Israelites" (2 Kings 21:2). He rebuilt the heathen altars and idols his father had torn down, turned the Lord's Temple into a heathen temple, sacrificed his own son by fire in a pagan religious ceremony, and practiced sorcery and divination with mediums and spiritists. His epitaph said that "Manasseh led the people astray, so that they did more evil than the nations the LORD had destroyed before the Israelites" (see 2 Kings 21:9).

Was fifteen more years of a king's life worth all the evil that ensued? If Hezekiah had died sooner rather than later Israel's treasure wouldn't have been exposed. Manasseh wouldn't have been born.

Did God make a mistake in letting Hezekiah live? Or in appointing Saul king? Does all this mean that God is less than kind? No on all counts.

The stories of Saul and Hezekiah show us that God *can* say *yes* to less than best. From the human side of history, certainly, it looks like Saul should never have been king and that Hezekiah would have been better off dead. But we can't grasp the mysteries of God's mind.

God knows the end from the beginning. He sees the future that we cannot see. He foresees exactly where history is going and masterfully brings jagged pieces together to fit his design, knowing how even the worst of turns could still help fulfill his ultimate purposes. Even the hardships that result when he says *yes* to our less-than-best requests have their place in his plans.

No to Prayers That Aren't in Our Best Interest

I am embarrassed to admit that most of my prayers are *selfish*. I know it. I wish they weren't. I try to be less selfish but find that hard to do. I slip back into self-serving patterns. Frankly, even my seemingly unselfish prayers for others often have a twist that serves my purposes. I pray for the marriage of two friends to improve, for example, knowing that my life would be happier if they didn't divorce.

God is gracious when he filters the selfishness from what I ask before he answers. He doesn't try to escape his promise to hear and answer my prayers. Instead, he cares enough to fix my prayers before he answers them. While I know this in theory, I struggle with it in reality. It too often irritates me that God doesn't give me what I want in exactly the form I request. I usually prefer that God do it my way rather than his better way.

The strange thing about selfishness is that we can't clearly see it in ourselves. The only eyes through which we can see and interpret life are our own. You can persuade me to look from a different angle—but I will never see through anything but my own eyes. So I can't self-regulate. Without outside, objective help I sink in a self-dug hole of self-centeredness. It is the chronic problem of every sinner.

Praying with others is a practical correction to selfish prayer—which is why Jesus said that "if two of you on earth agree about anything you ask for, it will be done for you by my Father in heaven" (Matthew 18:19). This is a powerful but not unconditional promise. Two are less likely to be as selfish as one, but they can still ask amiss.

The ultimate solution is God. We trust him to see what we can't see. We believe he will answer our prayers for his and our best interests. It's like the dialogue between a private pilot flying cross-country and an air traffic controller at the FAA Denver Center. The pilot from the flatlands requested permission to drop to a 10,000-foot altitude. The controller repeatedly denied permission. While it seemed like a perfectly reasonable request to the pilot, who lived near sea level, the controller knew that the mountains in his flight path were more than 14,000 feet high. The pilot didn't want to crash—he just operated from limited experience on different terrain. What made sense to him really made no sense at all. So it is with God, who often denies our requests of what we misguidedly think is best for us.

If God gave us everything we selfishly seek we would soon self-destruct.

Related to blind selfishness is the *quest for ease*. Many of our prayers ask God to lead us down the easiest path in life. Who wants God to make life hard? I suppose it was the naturally human part of Jesus' prayer that the cup of the cross be bypassed. Humans are designed to shun pain, and crosses are always painful.

But the easy way is often neither the right way nor the best way. Just as cutting a butterfly from its cocoon may make escape easier but leave its wings too weak to fly, the easy alternatives too often leave us unprepared for all God has purposed in our lives.

Take a survey of any Christian group. Ask, "When in your life were you closest to God—and when did you most grow spiritually?" With few exceptions the answers will be "during the hardest times." Imagine what our lives would be like with no struggles or pain. Does a problem-free existence sound delightful? It might not be worth living. We would be consumed with pleasure, believe we are self-sufficient, immerse ourselves in self-indulgence and never know God.

Suffering has great benefits: "Suffering produces perseverance; perseverance, character; and character, hope" (Romans 5:3–4). When suffering is understood from God's perspective it becomes a source of joy: "Rejoice that you participate in the sufferings of Christ, so that you may be overjoyed when his glory is revealed" (1 Peter 4:13). Suffering not only builds character but also gives us a solidarity with Jesus Christ, who suffered for us. Character and Christlikeness are far better than comfort. Knowing all this, God may often say *no* to our comfort-seeking prayers in order to preserve the greater benefits of suffering.

Suppose that a parent removed every obstacle from a child's path, prevented all discomfort and complied with every whim. A child would play with fire when he was two, rot his teeth with candy at seven, maim himself with cars at eleven and squander the family fortune at the beach when seventeen. What a child that parenting would produce! In popular terms, a spoiled brat. In theological terms, a complete reprobate. In personal terms, a totally miserable individual.

True. All true. We know it's true—but we still pray for the easy way. I don't criticize those who seek ease. I do it myself all the time. (I would be more worried about the masochist who enjoys pain.) When we pray for the easy way God answers with greater love than the kindest earthly father. He loves us too much to allow easy lives. He says *yes* to enough requests for ease that we don't become completely discouraged and *no* to enough requests that we don't turn into ungodly and undisciplined brats.

We also are prone to pray for *speed*. Humans and God live by different clocks. Because our lives typically last a short three score and ten years we burst with an internal pressure to have everything immediately. The eternal God who never began and will never end isn't in as much of a hurry.

North Americans have quickened life's pace to an all-time

high. We have more experiences in childhood than most people have in a lifetime. But we keep cramming in more. We are shaped by an age of instant gratification—we want products and pleasures and proficiencies sooner rather than later. And ten minutes later we expect something more and different. Our generation has reduced life's problems to television dramas where the most profound issues are raised and resolved in less than an hour.

I like the story of Americans who hired African nationals to carry their supplies on a long journey through difficult terrain. Each day the Americans pressed the laborers to walk faster, work longer and travel farther. Finally the entire crew sat down and refused to continue. They explained that they had to wait for their souls to catch up.

It is presumptuous to think that God should change his pace to fit our calendars. Not that he is slow or lazy—he is wise and experienced. He not only knows what to do but when to do it. The better way is for us to set our pace by him rather than beg for the other way around.

When God says *no* he often is slowing us down. At other times he speeds us up. Either way he is good enough to recognize when our prayers aren't in our best interests and to tell us that through his negative response to our requests.

No to Give Us Something Better

Garth Brooks' hit recording "Unanswered Prayers" is about young romance reconsidered at a high school reunion. God had graciously said *no* to a request for a lifetime with his high school sweetheart. Brooks explains on the album cover that "this is probably the truest song I have ever been involved with as a writer. This actually happened to my wife and me when we went back home to Oklahoma. Every time I sing this song, it teaches me the same lesson . . . happiness isn't getting what you want, it is wanting what you've got."[2]

It's good when God says *no* in order to give us something far better than we were smart enough to ask.

There are times when *no* is the best answer God can give. That doesn't mean our prayers flow from shortsighted or evil motives. It's just that God knows so much better. What God doesn't grant is rooted in his overflowing wisdom. Prayer itself is an acknowledgment of our inferior and God's superior position. If we always knew best there would be no need for God or prayer.

On the Mount of Transfiguration, Peter, James and John witnessed a rare and spectacular unveiling of supernatural splendor. For one brief moment the glory of Jesus Christ was revealed for human beings to see. It was as if Jesus' earthly disguise was taken off and he appeared in his God-clothes from heaven. Moses and Elijah supernaturally appeared from the other side of the grave and conversed with the transfigured Son of God. While this may have been routine fare for heaven it was stunningly unique on earth. Peter, James and John had no idea how to react.

Peter impulsively blurted out a prayer. It was not well thought through. He spoke more from fear than faith. He said to Jesus, "Rabbi, it is good for us to be here. Let us put up three shelters—one for you, one for Moses and one for Elijah" (Mark 9:5). Jesus never answered Peter's prayer. Peter quickly understood that no answer was a *no* answer.

God had something far better than a memorial shelter in mind. He sent a cloud that enveloped them all and the Almighty God of heaven spoke out loud: "This is my Son, whom I love. Listen to him!" (Mark 9:7).

Which was better—to scrounge around for some branches to mark the spot or for God to break the silence between heaven and earth and make his voice heard to the disciples? When the privileged men walked with Jesus down the mountain the shelters were never mentioned again.

Mary and Martha were counted among Jesus' closest friends. He turned them down as well. It was a life-and-death situation.

Their brother Lazarus was dying and they knew his last hope was a touch from Jesus. The sisters sent an urgent message to Jesus telling him that his friend was sick and that Jesus needed quickly to come to Bethany. The record of Jesus' response to their request seems contradictory: "Jesus loved Martha and her sister and Lazarus. Yet when he heard that Lazarus was sick, he stayed where he was two more days" (John 11:5–6).

When Jesus says *no* to our prayers it does not mean that he loves us less. True love can give surprising answers.

By the time Jesus finally arrived he surprised them again, saying, "Lazarus is dead, and for your sake I am glad I was not there, so that you may believe" (John 11:14). Needless to say, Mary and Martha were disappointed with Jesus. When they first talked to Jesus after his arrival each of them said, "If you had been here, my brother would not have died" (John 11:21, 32). The scene has been reenacted and the words rephrased many times in the centuries since. Many friends of Jesus have sent for him when those they loved were sick or dying. When Jesus didn't come or arrived too late they too were disappointed—disappointed not just in the outcome but disappointed in Jesus. They have doubted his love and told him that "if he had been there" everything would have been different.

It wasn't that Jesus didn't care. He cried so sincerely and profusely that even strangers knew he loved Lazarus. Jesus simply had a greater cause. And Lazarus was part of it.

Jesus raised Lazarus back to life, proving to his generation and all of history that he held the ultimate power over the grave.

Think how different everything would have been if Jesus had come as requested and healed Lazarus from his illness as expected. It would have been wonderful. But not good enough. Strange as it sounds, it would have been just one more miraculous healing. More important, history would have seen one less person raised from the dead. We often ask "what if?" when our prayers are declined. What if God hadn't said *no*? Here we have to ask a different "what if?" What if Jesus had said *yes* to the sisters' prayers? No doubt Lazarus would have been disappointed if he ever found out what he missed. He received something better.

Peter, James, John and Andrew were turned down as a prayer group. Isn't it interesting that we think God is more likely to say *no* to our private prayers than to our corporate prayers? Yet God declines and defers both individuals and groups without partiality if our prayers aren't for the best.

These four followers came to Jesus in premeditated group prayer. They asked him for a specific date when his predicted destruction of the Jerusalem temple would take place. He gave them plenty of information, but he never answered their question the way they wanted. They said, "Tell us, when will these things happen?" (Mark 13:4) and he answered, "No one knows about that day or hour, not even the angels in heaven, not the Son, but only the Father" (Mark 13:32). The information they requested, in other words, was secret and he couldn't tell them.

It isn't hard to guess why God keeps some information secret. If we knew when prophesied events would take place we wouldn't "Be on guard! Be alert!" as Jesus commanded (Mark 13:33). If we knew how and when we would die our stewardship of life might be ruined—we would be tempted to live sinfully and recklessly with illusions of immortality.

Recent research in genetics unveils information that has been hidden from all previous generations. It's foreseeable that lab tests will be able to predict characteristics of future children and forecast future diseases. They will foretell life expectancy with great precision. Most people have already concluded they don't want that kind of information. It's better to live ignorant of some things. Jesus knew that. He graciously granted ignorance of the divine timetable rather than burden his four friends and all future generations with data we aren't equipped to handle.

God Knows Best

The prayer of a righteous man is powerful and
effective.

James 5:16

We imagine that if our prayers are granted and our lives are extended everything will fall into perfect place and we will live happily ever after. It may seem merciless when God says *no* to our most passionate prayers. In reality his firm *no* may be the kindest word of all.

Still, we may doubt the power and effectiveness of prayer if God often tells us *no*—unless we better understand the meaning of faith and prayer.

The ultimate issue of faith isn't whether we get the gift we seek, but whether we trust the Giver to be good. Faith isn't about answers. Faith is about God.

Do we believe that God is wise, good, powerful, just, generous, holy and kind? If we really believe God to be all he claims to be, we know that he must always act consistently with his character. When our prayers violate God's character we shouldn't expect him to change to what we want. He would be a worthless and fickle God if he did.

There is great comfort in knowing that God cares enough to say *no*. Rather than suffer prolonged disappointment we can rejoice in the character of God.

So are we wrong to be disappointed when we are turned down? Is there something improper in us when we feel anger rise against God? Should we not press for an explanation when our convictions seem trivialized by God's silence to our pleas? All of these questions and reactions are common among Christians. After all, we wouldn't pray if we didn't believe—and we wouldn't believe if we didn't think prayer would make a difference.

God is like a strong and benevolent parent with a growing and changing child. The boy asks for something he deeply desires and expects to get. The boy is convinced that his father will immediately grant his wish, and when he is turned down the boy may feel rejected and lash out in anger against the person who loves him most. It is one of the great contradictions of humanity that a child says "I hate you" to the parent he loves more than anyone else in the world. The child knows deep down that refusal is not rejection, that anger indeed hurts but it never causes a devoted parent to stop loving, and that Dad and Mom in the end will probably be proven right. A sure sign of a healthy family is that relationships are more important than things.

When God says *no* he hasn't rejected us. He loves us no less. We know that in the end he will be shown to be right. Our faith is in God, not the things we hope to receive. Our relationship to him is the best gift of all.

Submitting to God's Best

You are wiser than I could understand. Your schedule is always on time. You see all the pieces and how they fit together. You are constantly kind.

Thank you for hearing my prayers with such great patience. You listen to requests that are crazy and do not laugh. You treat me with such respect when I am so selfish and in such a hurry.

I really believe that you know best. Even though I often pray as if I know better and sound like I'm telling you what to do, I know deep in my heart that I don't come close to comparing to you.

Please don't say yes to my stupid prayers.

Please protect me from my ignorance, impatience and selfishness.

I want to go on record once and for all that I submit to your greater wisdom and better timetable. As best I can, I will accept your no with grace because I am absolutely convinced that you always have my best interests at heart. You are great and you are so very good.

Thank you, Lord. Amen.

Notes

1. Augustine, *Confessions* (8:6–12) from David Hazard, *Early Will I Seek You* (Minneapolis: Bethany House Publishers, 1991), pp. 42–46.
2. Quoted from the cover of *Garth Brooks / The Hits* (Nashville: Capitol, 1994).

THREE

Opposite Prayers Do Not Attract

Everett and Dory Healy know how to pray. Loving, compassionate and godly, they are people I want praying for me when I face life's deepest crises. Their friend in Wisconsin must have been specially blessed when the Healys came to visit her in the hospital and to pray for her healing. Their friend suffered from a malignant brain tumor that had already robbed her of her ability to walk.

The Healys prayed specifically that Marion would recover and be restored to her family and friends. One day later she went into a coma. She was unable to move any muscles, eat on her own or control body functions. Week after week the coma persisted, and after six months her doctors said she would never recover. Every noon her husband visited her to try to feed her, with no response. Family and friends began to pray that God would mercifully take her home to heaven. At least twice a day the Healys asked God for her life to end. They phoned often to keep updated on the friend they loved.

There were no changes. After a year Marion was still in a deep coma. The Healys continued to pray "God, please take her home." Then the Healys received news from their friend's elated husband. Marion had suddenly awakened! She was alert, knew everyone by name, was happy, hungry and wanted to see all of her family and friends. "God didn't answer our prayer as we had prayed," Everett Healy says. "Like our heavenly Father often does, he had a better plan in mind."

We pray for one thing. God grants another. This kind of contradiction is one of prayer's ironies. But there is a second, related contradiction that happens often in prayer. When dozens of people pray for something it seems inevitable that the prayers won't be *identical*. We pray in different directions. Not only that, it seems probable that when a group of people prays that some prayers will be altogether *contradictory*, with different people asking for opposite answers. When a friend is sick some pray for a peaceful death, a quick and merciful welcome to heaven's home. We know that others continue to pray for recovery, believing healing in the here and now to be God's best. Even a solitary individual may change his mind and stop praying for one thing and start praying for another—or flip-flop between two opposing prayers.

God somehow must reconcile all the concerns we voice. And someone somewhere receives God's *no* for an answer.

The weather is a ready example of contradictory prayer. During the summer drought of 1989, sixty-five percent of Iowans prayed for rain.[1] But while a farmer prays for rain to end the drought and save his crop, a vacationer prays for dry skies and gentle winds. A mayor wants enough precipitation to refill the dangerously low reservoir but not so much that roads and homes will be flooded. The Sunday school teacher petitions for a sunny, warm and dry Saturday for the annual church picnic.

Certainly God hears prayers about the *weather*. When Elijah prayed for rain it rained (1 Kings 18). When Jesus prayed for calm the storm stopped (Luke 8). We don't, however, expect

God to cause flood and drought at the same time and place. Rain sometimes falls on one side of the street while the sun shines on the other—about as close as we can get to contradictory prayers being granted. But such weather is usually a meteorological peculiarity rather than a supernatural answer to neighbors' quarreling prayers. Besides, most answers to conflicting weather prayers simply go one way or the other.

Add *sports* to the list of opposite appeals. Sports leave limited possibilities for outcomes: win, lose, maybe tie. There is no way for both sides to win. God can either answer one side's prayers, stay out of the game entirely or just make "his team" victorious. Yet we frequently watch sports contests where athletes on both sides pray in a huddle, kneel in the end zone after a touchdown, or cross themselves before stepping into the batter's box. Few admit on national TV that they pray for their teams to win—but it's a safe guess that they do. As silly as it makes me sound, I admit to having prayed to win racquetball games at the YMCA or softball games at church picnics.

It all starts to sound sacrilegious. Certainly God has more important things to do than determine the outcome of sports events—although another perspective argues that God is interested in the smallest details of our lives. If an earthly father cares about his son's soccer game the heavenly Father must care at least as much.

What about conflicting prayers for *national concerns and crises*? We offer prayers in spheres with much more at stake than a Little League trophy. Jimmy Carter admits that he prayed for Newt Gingrich and Oliver North to lose in the November 1994 elections (Gingrich won; North lost).[2] Certainly there were others who prayed they would both win.

When the *Apollo 13* mission was nearing disaster and death between earth and the moon, Congress passed a joint resolution urging everyone to pray for the astronauts.[3] With so many people praying how could there not have been prayers that differed and even disagreed?

The faithful of every religion pray on the eve of battle.

About sixty percent of Americans believe wartime prayers are effective.[4] The prayers usually revolve around two requests: personal survival and military victory. At the least, the praying soldier wants to survive. At the most, the praying soldier wants his side to win.

During World Wars I and II Christians often fought Christians. German believers prayed in the name of Jesus Christ for German victory. French, British and American soldiers pleaded for Allied victory, also praying in the name of Jesus Christ. Thousands of crosses in military cemeteries testify that Christians were casualties in large numbers on both sides. God said *no* and thousands died; God said *yes* and thousands lived.

Then there are the *highly personal prayers* of contradiction. He pleads with God to intercede in the finalizing of their divorce, asking for a change in her heart. She prays with equal passion that he will leave her alone, allow the divorce to go uncontested and accept that the marriage is dead.

If there are contradictory prayers that pierce the deepest human emotions and raise the highest of ethical issues, they are prayers related to transplantable human organs. The people involved seldom know each other. They would wish each other no harm. God hears the prayer of one forty-two-year-old mother outside a hospital emergency room: "Dear God, please save Hank's life. Stop the bleeding. Don't let his brain die. I promise he'll never ride a motorcycle again. I'll do anything you ask. Hank will do anything you ask. Just please, please, please, don't let my boy die." Five hundred miles away another forty-two-year-old woman stands by the bed of her son, who is dying from heart failure. She prays for a donor organ: "Dear God, we're running out of time. If Bill doesn't get a heart by tomorrow he'll die. Lord, I've done everything I know to do. It's up to you. Please find a suitable heart and get it here in time. Save my son's life." Good people. Sincere prayers. It can't be both ways. A heart can't be shared.

The most obvious reason God says *no* to our prayers is because he can't say *yes* to prayers that contradict.

Sometimes one person's requests are incompatible in the same prayer—maybe even in the same sentence of the same prayer. More often, two godly pray-ers ask God for opposite answers at the same time. We can't know everyone else's prayers, yet it seems reasonable to assume that ours aren't always answered as we wish because God must choose who gets *yes* and who gets *no.*

How strange that the Bible isn't full of such examples! The Bible, in fact, is empty of them. The silence of the Scriptures is strange if not confusing:

- Perhaps God has some supernatural and mysterious ability to reconcile contradictory prayers. In that case, what seems like a contradiction to us wouldn't be beyond God's ability to fulfill.
- Perhaps a contradictory prayer is an invalid prayer. It doesn't qualify as a prayer at all, so God automatically rejects them. Like a husband and wife who cancel each other's vote, contradictory prayers do not count.
- Perhaps the Bible is silent because the mystery reaches beyond our capacity to comprehend. God prefers that we pray appropriately and leave conflicting prayers for him to understand. If we try to resolve the contradictions we step over the line into divine prerogative.
- Perhaps contradictory prayers are so obvious that there was no good reason for the Bible's authors to waste space telling us what we should be able to figure out for ourselves.

Let's go with the final alternative—and assume that God isn't hiding something from us and that the Bible is silent because God expects we can figure this out without an explanation.

What should God do when he hears contradictory prayers? It's the problem every loving parent faces when children ask for opposites—only in God's case the stakes are infinitely higher.

What Is God to Do?

Suppose that contradictory prayers were won by merely human criteria:

- Who prays hardest
- Who prays longest
- Who has been a Christian for the most years
- Who has the most faith
- Who promises more
- Who sins less.

None of these characteristics are bad. All are part of the interpersonal and spiritual dynamic of prayer. It just seems prudent that God's answers to prayer be primarily based on his character and wisdom rather than the attributes of the person praying.

To pick up on earlier examples—suppose that a godly draftee in the Nazi army prayed longest, hardest, with the most faith, fewest sins and biggest promises. He asked for victory. But God knows that the ultimate right and good is an Allied triumph. If God were bound by a human point system he would be forced to say *yes* even though *no* is the better answer.

Would a mother in a hospital want the fate of her son determined by the seven years another mother has been a Christian compared to her own seven months of faith? Worse yet, should any twenty-one-year-old coma patient live or die based on the many sins or little faith of a relative whose prayers he can't even hear? Would it not be better if the final choice was made by a God who has never sinned and whose spirituality is ultimate?

God is the ultimate arbiter in every example listed and millions more every day. That is very precious news.

Contradictions That Get an Automatic *No*

When the president-elect of the United States takes the oath of office to become head of state he swears to uphold the

Constitution of the United States of America. He is oath-bound to say *no* whenever he receives requests contrary to the constitution, whether in a bill from Congress, an order from the Supreme Court, a petition with a million signatures or a note from a high school sophomore. To knowingly contradict the Constitution is an impeachable offense.

God holds himself to higher than human standards. His nature is consistent, his word is eternal and his standards are unimpeachable. In other words, it's a waste of time to ask God for anything that contradicts who he is or what he has said.

Do pray-ers really ask God to contradict himself? Sure. When prayers seek injustice or perpetuate untruth. When they lack love. We are glad God turns a deaf ear when the prayer is vicious and hateful. When a prayer ignorantly contradicts God's nature and word we can count on God to be compassionate—but his *no* is still *no*. Yet sometimes our prayers are so obviously contradictory to God's character that God must automatically refuse them. Those are prayers that deserve to be edited or deleted before they are sent.

God is consistent. That is one of the best things about him. Not that he has any choice, because consistency is in the essential nature of God. He doesn't contradict himself. All of his divine attributes perfectly and permanently mesh—holiness, knowledge, righteousness, justice, love, wisdom, eternality, power, presence, mercy and grace.

Yet *we* don't know all *God* knows. We may pray totally contradictory prayers out of ignorance more than arrogance. With our limited information and perspective, how are we supposed to know what to pray?

How Then Shall We Pray?

Is prayer a supernatural lottery? A hundred million pray—each with the hope of winning, each with the odds for losing. God can only award a limited number of prizes for contradictory prayers to work, so the winners will be few.

We have more hope than that. Our prospects would be bleak were God not full of surprises and grace. He can say *yes* to seemingly contradictory prayers, all because his answers aren't limited to our options.

God often answers the core of our prayer even when he seems to ignore the surface request. We may pray for dry weather to bring family members together in positive relationships. God turns a rained-out picnic into an opportunity for family togetherness that wouldn't have happened lying on a sunny beach. A farmer prays for rain to raise the best crop. God may use drought to push the farmer to plant a different crop that will prove far better.

Beware of underestimating God. He doesn't share our human fallibilities. He doesn't operate through inadequate human methods. Lotteries are tilted against the players. God is committed to us pray-ers.

God can't be underestimated even in life and death situations, though that is harder for us to believe. When a loved one dies there aren't many prospects for good to come. That is what Mary and Martha thought. But they were wrong. Jesus brought Lazarus back to life. But since that miracle seems unlikely for most of us, death appears to be the final *no*—unless we are convinced that God's aerial perspective of our lives and his history isn't limited to this lifetime. That takes great faith—to believe that God could answer our prayer for life with death and still capture the essence of what we asked. Christians are convinced that more of God's perspective and plan will be understood on the other side of death, when we have all been raised to eternal life (1 Corinthians 15). We may discover that God has answered more of our prayers with a *yes* than we had thought.

When prayers contradict, God serves as the judge who hears all the evidence and renders the final decision. He is fair and just. He will do right even if he is accused of doing wrong. He is willing to make the impossibly difficult decisions that are beyond our experience and wisdom.

His infinite capabilities may be hard for us to accept. Yet God is both more complicated and more capable than we will ever understand. Imagine a thousand people being exposed to the same virus—some are unaffected, some become slightly sick, some turn desperately ill and others die. From our perspective the disease seems random. Senseless. But there *are* variables determining the outcome: part of the thousand was in good health while part was sickly and more vulnerable; hundreds may have been exposed to the virus earlier in life and developed an immunity they never knew they had; one segment of the thousand may possess a genetic predisposition that puts them at higher risk for fatality than the majority; some had greater exposure than others without either group knowing how much.

My point is that what seems senseless may simply be beyond our knowledge. We cannot know or process all the variables. How unlike God! He takes millions of factors into consideration and always decides wisely, fairly, justly, lovingly and consistently—even though we often can't know all the variables converging into the divine decision.

God will make no mistakes.

Imagine if it were any other way. We would live in a world of spiritual nonsense and constant injustice.

When God says *no* to our most important prayers, there may be no explanation or rationale that our emotions will quickly accept. But if God is God, it is he who must set the priorities and not we. He sees the future in advance. He knows the end from the beginning. Only God can know that the son who died would have lived a painful life and borne no children. He is far better off in heaven than on earth. Only God can know that the son who lived would have a child whose grandchild would be God's leader for some great movement that would accomplish divine purposes on earth and reap eternal benefits in heaven. There is no way any mother could have this information or appropriately integrate it into her thoughts and prayers.

Not that prioritization is easy for God. He has feelings as well. He comprehends the pain of his decisions. Remember that Jesus denied the requests of Lazarus' family for Jesus to come and heal the dying man. Jesus gave greater priority to staying where he was than going where he was summoned (John 11:6). Jesus remained distant and silent for two days as Mary and Martha prayed for their brother to live and then watched him die. Jesus determined that there was a priority higher than life, that saying *no* was "for God's glory so that God's Son may be glorified through it" (John 11:4). When Jesus finally showed up in Bethany his friend was dead and Jesus wept. His grief was so great that the professional mourners present observed how much he loved Lazarus. He had a higher priority than Lazarus' life, but that made the choice no easier.

I assume the same is true when God says *no* to us. When his children's prayers contradict each other and he must choose one instead of the other, he weeps over the hurt his decision causes. He loves those to whom he must say *no* and shares their disappointment. Just as Jesus was reproved for his seeming insensitivity ("Could not he who opened the eyes of the blind man have kept this man from dying?" John 11:37), God's modern prioritization of prayers draws severe criticism from those he loves.

An Aerial Perspective

In 1994, television networks featured the fiftieth anniversary of the allied invasion of Normandy, called D-Day. They rebroadcast actual film footage and commentary from the decisive battle. The advantage of a fiftieth anniversary is that viewers know who won; the original films, radio tapes and commentaries could only report current events and future hopes.

Part of the anniversary celebration was a reenactment by former soldiers who took part in the invasion. The celebrations were likely the last public expressions of memories for men now in their seventies and eighties. Some wore their half-century-old uniforms. Others parachuted out of vintage aircraft to relive old moments of fear, courage and glory.

One telecast ran two interviews. The first was with a soldier who fought the battle on the ground. "I was convinced there was no way we could possibly win," he reported. The other interview was with a pilot, who saw a much wider view of the conflict. "I was convinced," he said, "there was no way we could possibly lose."

God has an infinite aerial perspective. He sees everything that is happening and hears every prayer that is spoken. When those of us caught in the heat of life's conflicts radio to God that "there is no way we can possibly win" God confidently replies that "there is no way we can possibly lose." Of course, it is a response of faith to believe God's answer over our own experience. It is the same kind of trust needed by those who pray contradictory prayers and leave it to God to figure out which to accept and which to reject. We must accept that he sees what we cannot see, knows what we do not know, chooses more wisely than we can choose and will answer prayers in the best way. When his answers defy our sense and experience it becomes an act of faith to accept his perspective as always best.

It seems like the worst of irrational escapes to claim that God only answers prayers that are offered "according to his will." While more will be said about this in Chapter 6, understand here that all prayers are acts of faith. Faith requires both confidence and submission—confidence in God's power to act and submission to his infinite superiority. He is superior. His will must overrule our will. If it were the other way around, we would be God instead of God being God. Challenging as it may be, what is "best" doesn't apply primarily to us. It applies first to God. He sorts and answers our prayers based on what is best for him. What is best for God is in turn always best for us.

Our every prayer is potentially contradictory. We must ask

God to choose "according to his will." We have the privilege of petition and God welcomes our frequent communication and multiple requests. But like a child trusting his parents' care, we accept in advance that God will lovingly do what he knows and wills to be best.

Prayer to the Consistent God

God, without contradiction, you are amazing. One of your many attributes that attracts me to you is your consistency. In this you are so simple and straightforward; we are so complex and convoluted.

Thank you for making us all so different. I like being an individual. While there are problems, I am glad that each of us is sufficiently distinct that we are able to pray unique prayers, even if they contradict.

I don't seek to pray contradictory prayers. I regret that I am so often selfish in what I ask. It is true that I pray competitively, wanting to win over the prayers of others who ask the opposite. I ask your forgiveness for my selfishness, your tolerance of my contradictions and your grace to pray better.

But I sense that you would rather I pray any prayer than to stop praying for fear my prayers won't be just right. You graciously straighten out all of the conflicting favors your children seek, with patience and love and sympathy.

May our conversations be more frequent and our relationship more intimate. Then may I know your will, feel your emotions, catch your thoughts—so that my contradictory prayers may quickly be revised and I may pray what you want me to pray. Amen.

Notes

1. Eric Zorn, "Let Us Pray," *Notre Dame Magazine* (Autumn 1995), p. 44.
2. Ibid.
3. Ibid.
4. Ibid.

FOUR

What Is Prayer, Anyway?

When I was a little boy my mother stood with her arms around me each morning before I left for school and had me pray by memory the words of Psalm 19:14: "Let the words of my mouth, and the meditations of my heart, be acceptable in thy sight, O Lord, my strength, and my redeemer" (KJV).

As a teenager I experienced prayer more passionately. It was on a February holiday when my plans were shattered. Though what happened wasn't very important in retrospect or from an adult perspective, at the time it was life-encompassing to me. I was home alone, upset and disappointed. My emotions were a surprising mix of tears and anger and sorrow. A feeling of helplessness drove me to kneel and pray aloud by my bed—something I don't remember ever doing on my own before. I admitted to God that I was in rebellion against him and asked for help. It was a turning point in my life.

My adult prayers have been too numerous to count: early morning prayers in daily devotions

prayers late at night with sick children or waiting for teen-
agers
prayers with clear, direct answers from God
prayers that never seemed to be heard
thousands of routine prayers before meals
prayers carefully written in my journal
spontaneous prayers in the urgency of the moment
prayers alone
prayers in public.

One would think that the combination of time and practice
would make me something of an expert on prayer, yet I consider myself a novice at best. Writing about prayer is for me as
much quest for understanding as it is communication of dis-
covery.

Could it be that many of the prayers I prayed weren't really
prayers at all? When God didn't answer as I expected, was it
because I never asked as I should?

No Isn't *No* When Prayer Isn't Prayer

Personal experience says that God may not have said *no* to
my prayers as often as I have thought. He may have said nothing
because he heard nothing. Not that God is deaf or ignorant—
but our prayers are really not prayers. What we call praying may
often be little more than thinking or talking to ourselves. What
is prayer, anyway?

Dictionary definitions of *prayer* aren't much help. The
books about prayer on my shelf always seem to assume that the
reader knows what prayer is before the first page. Prayer is more
than asking, although most prayers ask God for something.
Prayer includes adoration, worship, confession, meditation,
submission, intercession, thanksgiving, listening and even silence. Crafting a definition that covers such a broad range is
like writing a definition for love. Love and prayer are both defined better by experience than by words.

My own best short definition? *Prayer is communion with God.*

Communion Is More Than Communication

Communion is more than communication, although communication with God is the basis for all prayer. Answering machines and voice mail are communication, but rarely can they be considered communion. I have repeated communication with people who call my voice mail with a message—then I call back to talk to them through their voice mail—and then they call back and get my voice mail again. We exchange information. We experience personal thoughts and feelings. But it obviously isn't the same as voice-to-voice contact.

Communion here doesn't refer to a sacrament with bread and wine. Communion means communication that includes direct, close relationship. It is the wordless communication between a mother and the baby who nurses at her breast. The close bond between the best of friends. The conversation between a man and woman deeply in love.

Prayer is communion with God that expresses a relationship between God and the person who prays. "True, whole prayer," St. Augustine said, "is nothing but love."[1] When prayer rises to all it should be, prayer is love's expression. The love relationship is first; prayer is the communication channel for that love relationship. Perhaps we should not ask if our prayers are answered but if we love God and are communicating within that love!

Christians are people related to God through Jesus Christ. They enter that relationship through prayer and maintain that relationship through prayer. Like any interpersonal connection it has its ups and downs. We drift away from God when we sin and we come back through confession and forgiveness. But we draw close to God as we share with him the secrets of our hearts known to no other. God alone truly understands us and shares with us the heights of our joys and the depths of our sorrows.

Communion with God is intimate connectedness that is an indescribable mix of the relationship between a parent and child, between two passionate lovers, between best friends, between brothers and sisters, between monarchs and subjects.

Prayer is sharing this supernatural relationship not only in words but in thoughts and silence.[2] Prayer is the language of the soul with God himself.

I know that this definition and description of prayer is potentially discouraging. It is so far beyond the way we usually pray. The desperate person in crisis calls out for help to the Lord he barely knows. Does this invalidate the prayer? It might.

Compare our relationship with God to our other personal relationships. They start slowly and at a distance. Over time they either speed up and close in or are increasingly invalidated by distance. We have different expectations of a request made by a new employee compared to a veteran, a first date compared to a long marriage, a newborn child compared to a teenager who grew up in the home. We readily excuse clumsy communication if the relationship is new but expect more if the relationship is long-standing. God may excuse ignorance and insensitivity from the unbeliever or new Christian, while expecting far more from the disciple who should know better. There is an inseparable link between all communication and relationships.

The best example of prayer as it is meant to be comes from Jesus.

Christian Prayer Is Patterned After Jesus

When all the people were being baptized, Jesus was baptized too. And as he was praying, heaven was opened and the Holy Spirit descended on him in bodily form like a dove. And a voice came from heaven: "You are my Son, whom I love; with you I am well pleased."

Luke 3:21–22

Crowds of people were being baptized in the Jordan River. Setting an example for his disciples, Jesus volunteered to be baptized as well—as our baptism identifies us with him, his baptism identified him with us.

Jesus' mind wasn't on the water temperature or depth. His focus wasn't on the crowd or what they were thinking about him. Jesus prayed—communing with God the Father through his baptism. Something stunning happened—heaven opened.

Prayer is like a key that opens heaven to us on earth. Prayer touches the heart of God through the two-way communion of love and relationship.

There is no record of what Jesus said when he prayed; perhaps his prayer was too private to share publicly. Perhaps it is because the words themselves were unimportant.

This is the pattern of prayer for Christians: we are to practice prayer as love communion with the God who opens heaven when we pray.

> Very early in the morning, while it was still dark, Jesus got up, left the house and went off to a solitary place, where he prayed.
>
> Mark 1:35

Mark records a fascinating insight into the private life and schedule of Jesus. He awakened *very* early in the morning—before sunrise—in order to pray alone.

This report is especially amazing given Jesus' agenda the day before. The previous page reports that Jesus preached in the synagogue, was publicly confronted by a man opposed to him, then expelled a demon from that man and was pursued by large crowds of people who pressed him to talk with them and heal them.

Most pastors will admit that they are emotionally and physically exhausted after preaching—Sunday afternoon naps are the norm for pastors' schedules. We all know what it does to us to be confronted by someone who dislikes us, especially if that person is filled with evil. It's absolutely draining. Jesus was as human as the rest of us. He must have been exhausted when he finally went to bed that night. Yet he rose "very early in the morning" to pray. It must have been hard. He must have been sleepy when he prayed.

Obviously prayer was a priority for Jesus too important to skip. The larger the demands on him, the greater his exhaustion, the more he needed to pray.

> Jesus often withdrew to lonely places and prayed.
>
> Luke 5:16

Jesus had another very busy and tiring day. The usual finale to such a day should be to relax and unwind or go to bed early. Jesus resisted those urges and found a private place to conclude his day with prayer. It isn't that Jesus didn't pray in public; he obviously did because the New Testament reports the words of his public prayers. Analyzing Jesus' priorities and schedule, however, shows his public prayers were only a small fraction of his praying. Most of Jesus' prayer communion with God was hidden in private. He once explained to his followers that "when you pray, go into your room, close the door and pray to your Father, who is unseen. Then your Father, who sees what is done in secret, will reward you" (Matthew 6:6).

Jesus' private relationship with God fueled his public life. The habit of putting prayer first and finding privacy for prayer kindles the best of relationships with God and fuels us for everything else in our lives—everything from long hard days to evil challenges to sickness and even battles with demons. It is the pattern for Christian prayer.

> One of those days Jesus went out to a mountainside to pray, and spent the night praying to God. When morning came, he called his disciples to him and chose twelve of them, whom he also designated apostles: Simon (whom he named Peter), his brother Andrew, James, John, Philip, Bartholomew, Matthew, Thomas, James son of Alphaeus, Simon who was called the Zealot, Judas son of James, and Judas Iscariot, who became a traitor.
>
> Luke 6:12–16

Selecting the original twelve apostles ranks among Jesus'

most important decisions. The right choice included Peter, who declared Jesus to be the Christ; Matthew, John and James, who wrote much of the New Testament; and Thomas, who was transformed from a serious doubter into the apostle to India. These were the men who would take Jesus' good news to the world and to all future generations. The choice had to be right.

For the entire night before his final decision, Jesus prayed. It might surprise us that Jesus, with all his supernatural wisdom and power, would require such preparatory prayer. His example should jolt us awake. We make our major decisions with far less wisdom and power—and therefore need at least as much preparatory prayer.

I am impressed when I hear Christians say, "I must pray first" before deciding about employment, marriage, business contracts, medical care and other life-shaping choices. All night prayer could be good, although we expend those energies much more readily for our hospital crises than our coming decisions. The pattern Jesus set for his disciples was to pray *before* we choose, nurturing all decisions in the context of communion with God—rather than appear to treat God as an appendage and rubber stamp to the decisions we make independent of his counsel.

"Lord, Teach Us to Pray!"

As we ponder the definition of prayer as "communion with God" thousands of thoughts ricochet through our minds—especially when we look at the prayer pattern of Jesus. We wonder if our first prayer shouldn't be the disciples' plea, "LORD, teach us to pray" (Luke 11:1).

Their request grew out of watching and listening to Jesus pray. They realized that he really knew how to pray! Jesus' prayers were intimate, powerful and effective. He was truly in touch with the Father and they wanted to experience what they saw Jesus experience.

Prayer is much more than speaking a request to God, telling him what we want done. In some cases, such an approach is more than inappropriate—it is audacious and offensive, like asking a rich stranger to hand you a million dollars. You have no relationship with him, no claim on him. He merely has what you want.

Millions of prayers may not be prayers at all. They are wishful thinking. They are selfish demands. They have little or no concern for who God is or what God wants. They do such damage they are better left unsaid. These are not prayers to which God says *no*; they are not prayers in the first place. What they lack is any understanding or effort to commune with God. If there is no relationship there is no prayer.

This harsh assessment probably doesn't apply to you. Anyone who cares enough to read a book about how God says *no* to prayer is a person who regards and relates to God. Godly Christians risk reading my criticisms above and begin to doubt that they have ever prayed a valid prayer. Where there was concern, there could now be despair. One of the dangers of prophetic forthrightness is that the least appropriate persons take the prophetic word most to heart and those for whom it is intended miss the point. So don't begin praying with a fear that your prayers aren't prayers. Begin with a desire to commune with God. Grow all prayers out of that communion.

There is an old story that has been passed around for so many generations that its accuracy is impossible to document. Even so, its point is valid even if the stuff of the story is more legend than history. It tells of a young soldier caught in the forest away from his army's camp on the night before a major battle. The sentries who arrested him assumed he was secretly meeting with an enemy spy to reveal military secrets. The young soldier was brought before the commanding officer for a summary court marital and probable execution for treason. The soldier's only defense was that he went into the woods to be alone to pray. A weak excuse, the officers thought. The commander sarcastically ordered the soldier to kneel and pray, jeering that he would need all the prayer he could get before he was shot. The young man knelt and prayed aloud with passion and eloquence while his superiors watched and listened. As the commander listened to the soldier's prayer his mind was changed. The soldier knew how to pray—and when he finished, the commander ordered him to stand and dismissed all charges against him. "If you had not often been on the drill field," he declared, "you would not have been able to perform so well under the fire of battle."

The young soldier had firmly established his communion with God many times before. When a life-threatening crisis loomed he prayed what really was a prayer. Ironically, he was probably better prepared for battle and possibly for death than anyone else in the army.

We can't use a one-time prayer-check to determine the true quality of our praying. We discover if our prayers are real prayers when we live in a relationship with God. As we commune with Him every day amid all of life's circumstances we build a close relationship. We develop clear channels of communication. When we make a request of God we are expressing our relationship, not seeking favors.

Does God Make Exceptions?

What if a person doesn't know what real prayer is? What if she is a new Christian when the crisis comes and hasn't had time to develop a mature relationship with God? What if he isn't a believer at all—yet blurts out, "God, help me, please!"? Will the Almighty ignore those less-than-perfect prayers because they fail this high standard?

Extreme answers are easy. Extreme answer #1 says that "God is God. He sets the requirements. If we miss the mark we're out. We have no right to claim anything from God that falls short of his demands. The answer is *no*." Extreme answer #2 says that "God is a God of outrageous grace. He is so gracious that his generosity often offends our sensibilities. God grants urgent prayers of unqualified pray-ers. His grace is far too big to worry about the inadequacy of a prayer. The answer is *yes*."

The truth lies in the middle. God has as much right to reject prayer that isn't prayer as we have to not answer a stranger's sales call during dinner. God is also outrageous in his grace, causing the life-giving rain to fall on the righteous and the unrighteous (Matthew 5:45). He wisely decides each case. What may seem inconsistent to us is fully consistent in the mind of God.

It is foolish for an unbeliever or an immature Christian to intentionally continue to pray inadequate prayers, hoping for more divine exceptions. When God's intent is to draw us into communion with himself through granting our requests, it would be sad to develop a strategy of unbelief or immaturity and expect God to keep doing whatever we ask.

Prayer is always meant to be a means of communication within relationship, with asking being only part of the communication. Prayer lets us worship God, love God, hear God, confess to God and submit to God—not just make requests of God.

An Answer Better Than *Yes*

What if I pray and God says *no* but my relationship with God improves? Could this be an answer better than *yes*? Many people frankly admit that they would rather get what they want than get God. A few would sell their souls to the devil if that's what it took.

God is the Christian's greatest joy, even when he says *no*. Sharon Madison is an editor by profession, a wife by marriage and a Christian by commitment. Like many of us Sharon has struggled with God's turn-down of her prayer request.

Sharon refers to Lloyd C. Douglas's book *The Robe*,[3] in

which a female character has an illness the Lord doesn't heal. When the character is asked if she is angry or bitter about God's refusal she replies that she feels just the opposite. A miraculous healing naturally would have caused her to thank and praise Jesus. She instead came to the point where she was able to thank and praise Jesus even without the healing. The result was a closer relationship with her Lord and a stronger faith in Him. Sharon says, "I'll add joy to that list of things I have gained by *not* getting what I wanted. I was in poor health for many of my early years as a young wife before being diagnosed with multiple sclerosis on my fortieth birthday. Along with frequent migraine headaches and other physical problems, this at first seemed like too much to bear.

"I determined in my heart that I would be miraculously healed. I even prerehearsed the wonderful testimony I would share about the power and love of God.

"I read books on healing. I knelt at the altar in church and prayed for it. I was anointed with oil and prayed for by the elders, as Scripture instructs. I even went to the church of a man famous for his gift of healing when our family was on vacation in that state. The 'healer' happened to be out of the country at the time.

"Then, when no healing or improvements came, I began to feel guilty. I thought that I hadn't followed God's formula for healing closely enough. I confessed every sin I could ever remember committing, asking God's forgiveness for anything that could be blocking His precious gift of healing.

"When the feelings of failure and guilt on my part became heavier instead of lighter, I began to doubt my faith. I questioned all the beliefs I had so wholeheartedly leaned on since becoming a Christian at age nine.

"If God is truly all-powerful and all-loving, why did He hold back an answer to my prayers? And the prayers of so many friends and loved ones who were concerned for me and my family?

"Just when secret despair was about to consume me, I

found a book on God's healing by Ron Blue. I read the whole thing, but the one point that jumped out at me was that being healed or not is not my responsibility—it is God's. There is no scriptural formula to follow to the letter in order to receive healing. Being sick is not my fault. In God's infinite wisdom and love, He'll decide what's best.

"Finally I was able to let go of the idea that if I was just 'good enough' God would heal me. What freedom I felt! A heavy burden lifted from me that has been replaced by God's joy.

"I spent some time a while ago with a couple who were new friends to me. The husband later commented to his wife that even though he knew I was in pain, he saw that I radiated joy. He was surprised. I'm not. The joy is there because I can trust God through anything, not depending on His 'yes' answer to my prayers. After all, He loves me!"

In communion with God, Sharon discovered an answer better than *yes*. That is prayer at its very best.

Desiring God

You are the One I desire, God. You mean more to me than all the answers to all the requests I could ever be granted. I long to know you better. I think of you again and again every day. I love to discover new expressions of who you are. I am thrilled to know you more and more.

Please forgive all the times I have tried to use you. I admit that often I have treated you as if you were created for me rather than I created for you. I recall too many "prayers" that were completely centered on me and what I wanted and barely thought about you or what you wanted. I just wanted to get out of you what I could. I am sorry.

Most of all, be my God. Then out of our relationship with you as Sovereign and me as subject, teach me to pray. Teach me when to speak and when to listen. Teach me to enjoy you and our communion in silence. Teach me to take greater delight in getting what you want than what I ask. Teach me to ask what you desire to give and then to take greater delight in your answer than in my request.

May my prayers truly be prayers! Amen.

Notes

1. Quoted by Richard J. Foster in *Prayer: Finding the Heart's True Home* (San Francisco: Harper San Francisco, 1992), p. 1.
2. See Henri J. M. Nouwen, *The Way of the Heart* (San Francisco: Harper San Francisco, 1981) for the place of silence in Christian prayer, life and ministry, based on the discipline of silence among the Desert Fathers.
3. Lloyd C. Douglas, *The Robe* (Boston: Houghton Mifflin Co., 1942).

FIVE

Wrong Relationships Ruin Prayers

Husbands, in the same way be considerate as you live with your wives, and treat them with respect as the weaker partner and as heirs with you of the gracious gift of life, so that nothing will hinder your prayers.

1 Peter 3:7

Peter probably learned about hindered prayers the hard way. Imagine him coming home late one evening. It had been an exceptionally difficult day. The pressures of life aren't unique to modern times and not even apostles were exempt from the effects of stress.

When Peter arrived he said nothing to his wife, although she had been anxiously waiting to talk to him. He treated her as if she weren't there, plopping down in a chair and putting his head on the table. When she asked him what was wrong he didn't bother to answer her.

They had already invited company for dinner so it was too

late to have a quiet evening alone. She had worked much of the day preparing a special meal for Peter's friends. They were having fresh fish, something of a delicacy in those days before refrigeration. Since it was almost time to start cooking she asked Peter for his help. After all, he was a veteran fisherman who not only knew how to catch fish but how to clean and cook them as well. What she most needed was help with the firewood. It was too heavy for her to carry so she wanted him to bring it in and set it up.

Peter finally talked. It would have been better if he had kept quiet. His words were cutting and unkind. "You just won't let me get a minute's rest, will you? Can't you see I've had a hard day and that I'm exhausted? I've done my work today and you should have done yours. Cooking is for women to do. You're supposed to tend the cooking fire. I'm tired of doing everything for you. What's the matter with you, anyway?"

Many wives would have answered back. Peter's wife responded with silence. She dragged the wood to the fire. She cleaned and cooked the fish. She hardly spoke a word all evening.

When the company arrived Peter perked up. He was an extrovert who gained energy from being around others. The guests were great admirers of Peter. He was increasingly famous and his stories about the years with Jesus always captivated his listeners. He talked for hours about all Jesus said and did, about Peter's part and the joys of "the good old days."

One of Peter's guests was surprisingly serious when he said, "Peter, it seems to me that *these* are your good days! You have a good life with great memories, a wonderful wife and a godly family. Other Christians have been persecuted and died, but God has graciously allowed the two of you to live. Bless the Lord, my friend!" Peter had to agree; God had given him life when others had died and Peter's life was obviously blessed by the hand of God.

In many ways it was a good and memorable evening—except Peter acted as if his wife weren't there. He never spoke to her. He acknowledged her presence only when he had to. Peter was so caught up in himself and his conversations that she didn't seem to matter.

No doubt she felt hurt and rejected, but this wasn't the first time. Peter was Peter. Sad that a man so powerful in preaching and performing miracles was so insensitive to his own wife at home. But Peter never gave it much thought.

The guests finally left around midnight. Peter should have been exhausted and ready for bed, but he felt energized. While his wife cleaned up and went to bed alone, Peter went out into his back garden to pray. It was a warm clear night with a nearly full moon. There was enough light to see better than at dusk or dawn.

On his knees, Peter eloquently prayed. He addressed God as the "Great Lord of heaven and earth. The God of love and forgiveness. The Father of our Lord Jesus Christ." It seemed like knocking on a door that no one answered. Peter wasn't a patient man so he said it all again, only louder. Then his prayer moved on to the long list of requests he presented in the name of Jesus—salvation for his Jewish friends in Capernaum; healing for the rabbi's daughter in Nazareth; money to send to the poor Christians who had lost their homes and jobs in Jerusalem; ideas for a sermon he was planning to give at the Temple courtyard the next morning.

Peter prayed and prayed but he knew he wasn't getting through. It was like something was in the way. In a sense, God said *no* to everything he asked. In another sense it was as if the heavens were brass and God wasn't even listening. Nothing helped. Peter prayed louder and softer. He stood, he kneeled, he laid out straight on the ground. He recited the Lord's Prayer. Nothing helped.

Exhausted again, Peter was ready to give up and go to bed. It soon would be dawn and he would face another demanding day with little sleep. As he walked toward the house he asked God a simple question: "What's the matter?" This time he felt he got through to God. So Peter stepped back, sat down and listened. Nothing. He asked God to guide his thoughts as he rehearsed yesterday and the days before. He confessed every sin he could remember. He thought about everyone he might have offended. He couldn't seem to find the key. He wished he could awaken his wife and ask for her advice, but it was so late and she had been so quiet and tired. That started a whole train of thoughts about her. He loved her. He thanked God for her. But he admitted to himself that he didn't show her much respect. He didn't use his strengths to complement her weaknesses the way she used her strengths to bolster his weaknesses. He rarely asked her to pray with him or to simply celebrate the life God had given them to share.

Suddenly Peter saw everything in a new light. God had at last answered the prayer asking what was wrong with his prayers. Peter realized that his attitudes and actions toward his wife were getting in the way of his prayers. He resolved to change and prayed one more prayer before he went to bed— that God would help him treat his wife the way she should be treated. He didn't sleep long or well. When he awakened he greeted her warmly and asked her to forgive him for the poor treatment he had given her the night before. It was the beginning of several days of kinder words, helpful deeds and respectful attitudes toward his life partner. About a week later he asked her to pray with him and she did. Their prayers centered on gratitude to God for their lives, especially their life together.

The next time Peter prayed alone in the garden was several weeks later. Not that he hadn't prayed often in between, but this was the first chance for an extended conversation with God alone in the place where he had unsuccessfully tried to pray before. What a difference! It was like those old times with Jesus. Peter felt as if he was talking to his Lord face-to-face. The prayer was more like a dialogue. He talked again about his friends at Capernaum, the rabbi's daughter and the poor Christians in Jerusalem. He knew that God heard every request and that the heavenly answers were given then or were on their way. The channel was clear.

The next Sabbath Peter was preaching on the relationship between husbands and wives. His sermon was going to be part of a little book he was writing. Sitting at his desk, he wrote and rewrote words that someday would be included in the New Testament. They were words as much about unanswered prayer as they were about marital relationships, words forged in personal experience: "Husbands, in the same way be considerate as you live with your wives, and treat them with respect as the weaker partner and as heirs with you of the gracious gift of life, *so that nothing will hinder your prayers*"[1] (1 Peter 3:7).

Relationships are important to God. When relationships are wrong, he is reluctant to hear and answer our prayers. Our off-kilter relationships may be with a wife or husband, relative, neighbor or co-worker. The wrong relationship most damaging to prayer is a wrong relationship with God. If that relationship is bad enough, God may tell us not to pray until we start to obey.

"So do not pray. . . ."

God told the prophet Jeremiah not to bother praying as long as the people of Judah persisted in their disobedient relationship with him.

> So do not pray for this people nor offer any plea or petition for them; do not plead with me for I will not listen to you.
>
> Jeremiah 7:16

God was fed up with the nation of Judah. He had patiently blessed the people for generations, yet they increasingly rebelled against God. The whole nation had turned against God and done the things he told them not to do. Jeremiah publicly denounced the national sins of theft, murder, adultery, perjury and heathen worship.

God hadn't given up on Judah. He still loved the people.

He just knew that answering Jeremiah's passionate prayers for them would make Judah worse instead of better. To get their attention he had to deny prayers and let them suffer the negative consequences of their choices.

It's like a family where a beloved child turns against all the high values of both parents and repeatedly behaves in destructive ways. The prodigal shows up at home only to ask for money. Or he calls from jail asking for bail and help hiring a lawyer. The first few times the parents may say yes. But eventually they conclude that granting his requests further enables his misbehavior and self-destruction. The hard but kind thing to do is turn a deaf ear.

God takes relationships seriously. He has no intention of becoming an impersonal vendor of favors. He wants to give his grace in the context of friendship and fellowship. Because he is always the initiator and our outrageously generous creator, he gives without our asking and often grants our undeserved requests. God's desire is to win our hearts and allegiance with generosity. When that approach fails, though, we force God to say *no* until we recognize the importance of a right relationship with him and we take remedial steps toward him. It isn't that God wants full compliance or utter perfection before he will again answer our prayers. It's that he wants us to repent (meaning "to turn around and start in the opposite direction") before we can again benefit from his grace.

The head of an American denomination took me out to lunch and told a penetrating story about his long-established group of churches. They were in an obvious, long-term slide toward fewer churches, fewer members, lower income and sagging morale. The leadership hired a national consultant to study the denomination and make recommendations to stop the decline and bring renewal. After extensive study the consultant met with the denominational leaders. This is what he said: "From everything I have discovered, this denomination has fallen on such hard times that there is no reversal possible. In a few years you will be out of business. I have no recommendations that will help." Because it was almost lunchtime he suggested they adjourn the meeting and go eat. He started to walk out of the conference room, leaving a sobered group of leaders stuck in their chairs. One broke the silence. "Isn't there anything we can do?" he asked.

"The only thing I can think of," the consultant replied, "is that you get down on your knees and pray to God for forgiveness. Repent and plead for mercy." He then left the room. After minutes of silence one of the stunned leaders turned out of his chair to kneel on the floor and began to pray out loud. He confessed the sins of the denomination and pleaded with God for forgiveness and mercy. One by one every other leader in the room knelt and joined in this prayer. The prayer meeting was spontaneous and supernatural. It lasted a long time.

That was a couple of years ago. Since then the denomination has seen a wonderful turnaround, with spiritual renewal, numerical growth in the thousands, a series of new churches started and plans laid to double the size of the denomination in the next five years.

Once the relationship with God was made right, their prayers were heard and answered.

Prerequisites to Prayer

There are certain prerequisites to prayer we need to understand if we hope to have the kind of relationship with God that he desires.

Prerequisite 1: A belief in God leads the list. Hebrews 11:6 explains that "without faith it is impossible to please God, because anyone who comes to him must believe that he exists and that he rewards those who earnestly seek him."

It only makes sense that a prerequisite to prayer would be a belief in God. Why pray if you don't believe God exists? Wouldn't that be like sending letters to Santa Claus?

Yes, there are atheists and agnostics who sometimes pray to

a God they claim doesn't exist. Their prayers are like letters "to whom it may concern." Occasionally, to everyone's surprise, God answers those prayers. God doesn't answer *out of* a relationship but with a *desire* for a relationship, demonstrating his generosity. He hears the prayers even of those who deny him. But there is a difference in the way God relates to the atheist, agnostic or other non-Christian. God hears. He may answer. But he hasn't obligated himself in advance.

It's the difference between asking a stranger for a favor and asking your spouse. Marriage obligates us to another person in a way that we aren't obligated to strangers. God may graciously hear and even answer the prayers of those who aren't believers, but it is the prayers of those who believe in him he has obligated himself to both hear and answer.

Some Christians mistakenly think that the Bible's call for faith means believing God will answer a prayer precisely as it is requested. Faith isn't faith in an answer. It isn't faith in prayer. It is faith in God. Faith is the belief that the unseen God is real and powerful and personal. Faith is the basis for relationship. Only when a person becomes a true believer can he or she have a relationship that forms the basis for communication and petition to God.

Prerequisite 2: A relationship with God. Everything about prayer is based on relationship. Without a relationship with God we're just talking to ourselves. That relationship may be good or bad, new or old, close or distant, warm or cold. But *some* relationship is a prerequisite to prayer.

When Jesus' disciples asked him to teach them to pray, Jesus said, "Our Father who art in heaven. . . ." His very first words convey the relationship between those who pray and God, their Father. Jesus later told his disciples that when they talked to God they should be sure to mention his own name. To God, a personal relationship with his Son is the basis for a relationship with him and of access to him through prayer. That is why we pray "in Jesus' name."

Prayer is to relationship as swimming is to water. Without

water you can't swim. You can pretend, mimicking the motions on dry land, but you can't actually swim. Without a relationship with God our words are motions that go nowhere and accomplish nothing.

The better the relationship, the better the prayer. If we are alienated from God because of neglect or sin, our channels of communication will be weak or cluttered. If our prayer is frequent and our relationship strong, then prayer will be direct, intimate and effective. Fortunately, God constantly desires and works to make his relationship with us strong. For our part we have a responsibility to press on to God with a right motivation. We don't seek friendship with God for what we can get from God but for God himself. The relationship should be the end as well as the means. We should be satisfied with God even if he never grants a single request we make. It's when we know and love God for himself that we develop the intimacy that results in prayers heard and requests granted.

Prerequisite 3: Communication. Communication is the means of relationship. This prerequisite may seem so self-evident that it appears to be unnecessary. Actually, we can't do without it.

Prayer is communication. It isn't asking. How unfortunate when we use "ask" and "prayer" as if they mean the same thing. Asking is really a minor subcategory of our overall communication with God. When requests make up most of our interaction with God our prayers are distorted and positive answers from God unlikely.

"Caller ID" is a phone service that displays each caller's name and telephone number. People who subscribe to this service quickly learn to check who is calling before picking up the phone. A best friend gets a completely different tone of "hello" than an unfamiliar, irritating salesperson. The difference is relationship—extensive or minimal previous communication.

God responds like we respond. A prayer from a friend who calls often finds a more receptive response than a prayer from someone who communicates seldom or never. Prayer isn't magic. It isn't babbling memorized words that have become meaningless through ignorance or overuse. Prayer is communication rooted in a living friendship with God.

Prayer is multifaceted. Like any other relationship, it's happy at times and sad at others—sometimes calm and reasonable, sometimes emotional and unreasonable, sometimes loud and sometimes silent. The prayers in the Bible illustrate a range of expression:

In 1 Samuel 1:15, we find infertile Hannah's *prayer of desperation.* She "poured out her soul to the LORD." She was so emotional that she was almost kicked out of the temple because she appeared to be drunk when she prayed.

Psalm 88:1–2 is a *plea for God to listen:*

> O LORD, the God who saves me,
> day and night I cry out before you.
> May my prayer come before you;
> turn your ear to my cry.

Feeling that God may not be listening to prayers is nothing new. What happens today happened to Bible writers as well. We all know how frustrating it is to have something to say and sense that the person we want to hear our words is not listening to us. "O LORD, hear my voice. Let your ears be attentive to my cry for mercy" (Psalm 130:2).

Complaining is part of most interpersonal relationships and complaining prayers are surprisingly common in the Bible. Psalm 142:1–2 says,

> I cry aloud to the LORD; I lift up my voice to the LORD for mercy. I pour out my complaint before him; before him I tell my trouble.

Jeremiah is much more direct when he complains that God deceived him and set him up to be mocked by others:

> O LORD, you deceived me, and I was deceived; you overpowered me and prevailed. I am ridiculed all day

long; everyone mocks me.

Jeremiah 20:7

It seems audacious to complain to God. You would think such words would be edited out of the Bible so we wouldn't be encouraged to groan at God. There is, however, a far greater point that the Bible makes about the security of our relationship. A strong relationship sustains complaint and criticism. A healthy relationship allows us to speak our minds. God is certainly strong enough to take whatever we say and wise enough to understand the underlying motives of our hearts. Words and emotions that would be inappropriate and offensive if we had no relationship are acceptable and understandable in our good relationship.

And, of course, sometimes we voice *prayers of request.* Most relationships have a give and take that includes asking questions and making requests of each other. Certainly God makes many requests of us and it is fitting that we make requests of God. In Matthew 7:7–8 Jesus encourages us to "Ask and it will be given to you; seek and you will find; knock and the door will be opened to you. For everyone who asks receives; he who seeks finds; and to him who knocks, the door will be opened." What Jesus promises sounds like parents' parting words to an eighteen-year-old son or daughter going away to college: "If you need anything, ask us for it. If there's something you are looking for, let us help you find it. If you get stuck somewhere call home and we'll get you unstuck." Parents want to be asked. Parents want to help and give. God is our heavenly Parent who shares the same delight in his relationship with us. He adds further encouragement in Philippians 4:6–7: "Do not be anxious about anything, but in everything, by prayer and petition, with thanksgiving, present your requests to God. And the peace of God, which transcends all understanding, will guard your hearts and your minds in Christ Jesus."

Sometimes praying is *passionate:* "During the days of Jesus' life on earth, he offered up prayers and petitions with loud cries and tears to the one who could save him from death, and he was heard because of his reverent submission" (Hebrews 5:7). In the context of an unblemished relationship with his Father, Jesus prayed with powerful emotion, even with shouts and tears. Jesus got into his prayers—but never was he irreverent or rebellious. This isn't to say our prayers should or could be constantly passionate, but we might be stifling our prayers if they aren't at times as emotional as anything we ever say. When we shout or cry let us not lose sight of who God is, imitating Jesus' reverence and submission.

Sometimes praying is *silent:* Romans 8:26 describes times when we simply don't know what to pray and the Spirit has to do the praying for us. We come to the end of our words and silently allow the Holy Spirit to take up where we leave off.

All of these examples demonstrate that prayer always happens in the context of an interpersonal relationship with God. How we get along with God is mirrored in the relationships we have between husband and wife, parents and children, and the best of friends—sometimes passionate, sometimes silent, sometimes praising, sometimes pleading, sometimes comforting and sometimes complaining. Prayer communicates in many different ways, all within a relationship with God.

Praying Into a Right Relationship

The way to pray is to begin. Many of us pray little because we never get started. Or we don't pray because we know our relationship with God isn't good. We fear praying substandard prayers.

The person with a heart's desire for a right relationship with God will please God and work on maintaining and improving that relationship. Among Bible characters, David and Peter model well a close relationship with the Lord. God communicated often with David, and the rich intimacy they shared is revealed in David's Psalms. Peter was in the inner circle of disciples who were Jesus' best friends. Both David and Peter seem like unlikely candidates for such close relationships. David was a deliberate adulterer and murderer who provoked and offended God with his sins. Peter publicly denied that he knew Jesus, disassociating himself from the Savior in Jesus' most difficult hours. Frankly, I have struggled to understand how these two men could be such favorites of God when they sinned so deliberately and flagrantly. We see, however, that they had hearts for God—that is, they passionately desired a close relationship with their Lord even though there were occasions when they behaved completely opposite of what they believed. The overall pattern of their lives overpowered these awful exceptions.

For those of us who also have hearts for God, prayer is how we restore or strengthen the intimacy that produces effective prayer. However far we feel from God, we simply begin to pray from our hearts with the best words we can speak. It may not come out right, but God hears our hearts more than our words.

Ask any parent about the "right way" for a child to phone home and you will receive a blank stare. Parents who love their children know there is no right way. Day or night, long or short—they are glad to get a call. Sons and daughters can phone home when they have nothing special to talk about or when they face life's biggest crises. It's okay to call Mom and Dad to tell a joke or to cry, to dial direct or call collect. There just isn't a "right way."

So don't worry about getting prayer "right." God loves to hear from you—any time, any place, any topic. You can ask him for money, plead for comfort or just talk about what happened at the office during the day. Over the course of your relationship your prayers will run the range of every emotion, every issue and every thing. God has amazing tolerance. He understands. He welcomes. So don't ignore him. Don't miss out on him. Don't treat him as if he isn't there or is last on your list.

Turning *No* Into Intimacy

So what can you do when you hear a silent *no* from God because of a wrong relationship?

If the wrong relationship is with your husband or wife, ask God what to do to make that relationship good and obey what God says. Even if your spouse is unresponsive, do what is right by God.

If the wrong relationship is with another Christian, follow the procedure in Matthew 18:15–20. Go to the person alone and try to straighten it out. If that doesn't work, go back with another Christian as a helpful third party. If that doesn't work, go to the church for help righting the relationship. If you are the one who offended someone, ask for forgiveness and make restitution. In other words, do everything in your power to be on good terms with other people. For God this is a basic part of following him, crucial for a positive prayer life. When we are unwilling to make our relationships with each other good, our prayers will be hindered. Because God is the Father of all people he values the way we treat others; our relationship with God is impacted by our relationships to God's children.

If the wrong relationship is with God, believe that God wants to make it good. He reaches out to each of us with love and grace. He welcomes our acknowledgment of sin with the promise he will forgive anything we confess (1 John 1:9). He gives us his expectations in the Bible so that we will know what is right and seek to do right.

Breaking through the silence brought about by bad relationships happens when we have a heart for God, having made a decision and fanned a desire to love God with all of our passion. We know in advance that we won't perform to our own standards, much less to God's standards—but we really want to! Most important is this: that we *really want God*.

Jesus gives us a straightforward way of saying all of this. We are to

Love the LORD your God with all your heart and with

all your soul and with all your mind. Love your neighbor
as yourself.

> Matthew 22:37, 39

Remember that there is a catch to all of this. If we start out
with the primary desire of getting God to change his *no* to *yes*
so he gives us whatever we ask, we are doomed to failure. We
will never find the intimacy we seek if God is merely a means
to the end of getting what we want. That's using God, not loving God. The *yes* of God is a benefit, a side effect, of an intimate relationship with him. The irony is that the person who
truly loves God and shares in an intimate relationship with him
becomes far less concerned about getting positive answers to
self-initiated requests. When a person has a heart-to-heart
union with God, other things don't matter as much as they
once did.

Understand that we should never make God a means to get
what we want. Our desire is for God himself. When we have
him everything else falls into place.

All Right Relationships

*Right relationships mean everything to you, Wonderful God. You
hate the sin that keeps us apart. You loved us enough to send your
Son to straighten out the problems between us. You were willing to
suffer and die to have a right relationship with me. I am so grateful.*

*Now I want to have with you and others the kind of relationships
you desire for me to have.*

*I confess that I have been proud and self-centered. I have put my
selfish desires ahead of the needs of others. I have treated others as
objects to be used for my purposes. All of these are sin. Please forgive
me.*

*Show me wrong relationships in my home, job, church and com-
munity. Help me to do what is right to love and treat others as you
love and treat them.*

But most of all, I yearn for a right relationship with you. I want to have a heart for you. I do have a heart for you. Forgive my inappropriate desire to have a right relationship in order to get what I want from you. From today onward you are the goal of my life and the desire of my affections. I pray to you for more than what you can do. I desire answers to prayer as the product of our friendship, not as the reason for our friendship.

I love you for you, not just for the good you give to me.

I love you. Amen.

Notes

1. Emphasis added.

SIX

God Wills Something Different

Like many young girls she dreamed of being a mother when she grew up. "I spent much of my childhood taking care of my dolls, praying they would come alive, carefully bathing and 'feeding' them. At twelve years old I became a woman and remember thanking God, knowing that one day I would bear children. I felt happy, warm and contented."

But this Minnesota woman's dreams were not to come true. "When I was twenty-nine, after seven years of marriage, my husband and I were told there would be no children. Adoption was not an option—my husband felt 'unworthy.' I was devastated that my prayer was not answered."

But God had something different in mind for her. Now sixty-two years old, she reflects back with a mature perspective. She says that "God answered in a way we hadn't thought of— infant foster care—so many wonderful months of caring for newborns. Then, another answer to prayer—the adoption agency *asked us* to permanently care for a foster child who was then in our home. They *asked us* to adopt. My husband couldn't refuse. Thirty-two years later, I thank God for his answer to parenthood in his timing and in his way—two daughters and two grandchildren."

Jesus says we can ask for anything in his name and God will give it to us:

> I tell you the truth, anyone who has faith in me will do what I have been doing. He will do even greater things than these, because I am going to the Father. And I will do whatever you ask in my name, so that the Son may bring glory to the Father. You may ask me for anything in my name, and I will do it.
>
> John 14:12–14

> The Father will give you whatever you ask in my name.
>
> John 15:16

> In that day you will no longer ask me anything. I tell you the truth, my Father will give you whatever you ask in my name.
>
> John 16:23

As much as Jesus insists that this is the truth, many would disagree. They have prayed to God in the name of Jesus Christ—and *not* received what they asked. To Christians who believe they have met God's requirements, not hearing God's *yes* is faith-shaking. They counted on such a clear promise. God failed to live up to his end of the contract. It makes many wonder if God can be trusted or if anything else that Jesus says is true.

Yet there is further insight in 1 John 5:14:

> This is the confidence we have in approaching God: that if we ask *anything according to his will*, he hears us.[1]

The author who recorded the earlier quotes from Jesus is the same John who wrote this later expansion. Since there were years between the writings, John may have faced criticism from Christians who took Jesus' words at face value and were disappointed. In 1 John 5:14 he comes close to quoting Jesus, but he adds a condition: requests must be "according to his will" in order to be granted.

For some this answer may be enlightening. For many it is distressing. As Christians, we should want to please God in our prayers and not desire anything that God does not want. There is comfort in knowing God doesn't automatically grant us everything we seek. God would be continually granting wishes he opposes. On the other hand, the whole debate seems rooted in circular reasoning. If God only grants what he wants, what is the point in praying? Won't God do anyway whatever he desires? Can there be any proof of the power of God or the effectiveness of prayer if he only says *yes* when he agrees? Doesn't that make prayer a little too neat and safe? Every time we don't get what we pray for we can cover God's reputation by saying it must not have been according to God's will.

This is a serious issue for any Christian's system of belief. It can be an enormous problem of the heart for sincere Christians who feel frustrated by the knowledge that they can't fully discern God's best will until after they have prayed. It's enough to keep many from praying at all.

The Official Answer

Nineteenth-century American evangelist D. L. Moody once spoke to some of the children of Edinburgh. To seize their attention he started out with a question: "What is prayer?" He intended it to be a rhetorical question—a dangerous approach with children. Many children raised hands to answer, as if reciting in a school classroom. Moody called on a boy who stood up and said with a loud clear voice: "Prayer is an offering up of our desires unto God for things agreeable to his will, in the name of Christ, with confession of our sins and thankful acknowledgment of his mercies." To this Moody replied, "Thank God, my boy, that you were born in Scotland!"

I'm not sure the boy's ready answer came solely from living in Scotland, but he did recite the official catechetical answer to Moody's question as it was taught in the Church of Scotland (Presbyterian). For our prayerful requests to be effective they must be agreeable to God. God doesn't routinely grant requests he knows to be wrong, contrary to his values or antagonistic to his greater purposes.

If God didn't require that prayers be "according to his will" for him to answer *yes*, he would no longer be functioning as God. He would merely be the pawn of human prayers, or a machine whose powers are released by humans pushing the prayer button. The consequences would be far-reaching and disastrous. Prayers would be answered for help in robbery, rape, molestation and murder. Sinners would use prayers to break all of the Ten Commandments. Prayer would couple the worst of human sinfulness with the unlimited power of God. Not only would God be compromised, but we would be destroyed. The simplest of logic requires that positive answers to human prayers must be limited and controlled.

Most of us, however, aren't praying for skill to rob a bank or strength to murder an enemy. Our prayers usually seem consistent with everything we believe God wants. We pray for the peace of Jerusalem, the salvation of the lost, the healing of beloved friends, the health of Christian churches, the wisdom to make wise choices. How could any of these be contrary to God's will? And if they are consistent with God's will, why does God hesitate or refuse to grant our requests?

True Stories

True stories of men and women who prayed for one thing and received another are often powerful tales of the pleasant surprise of God's will.

A recent retiree, for example, prayed for God to make her son into a good student, which seems like an entirely appropriate prayer for a mother to pray. How could God see it any differently? The mother explains that "for years I begged, cajoled and lamented before God, asking him to make my son a good student. Quick with an acerbic remark, he kept his classmates and parents laughing and off guard. In second grade he did eighteen pages in his math book—for the whole year! His senior year in high school we held our breath waiting for him to graduate. One school accepted him for college. After three years and many classes, he left college. We hadn't paid for Ds and Fs, so he had to get a job to pay for many classes. For his hard work he was commended by customers. He rented apartments for a management company. This led to his pursuing a real estate license. He loved the classes and did well. Today he is a very successful real estate agent, father and Christian. He is a contributor to his high school and president of his alumni class. God never made him into a good student of academics— but rather into a man of high character. God gave him a great love for Christ and people."

This mother sincerely prayed for her reasonable will. God said no and gave her his own better will. The caring hand of God that was hard to see and believe at the time has become obvious now.

The same principle is written into Kathy Healy's story of pain and motherhood. Her battle with serious sickness began when she was fifteen and became chronically ill. "Over the next five years I had three major surgeries and spent close to 350 days in the hospital. It took the doctors some time to diagnose it. I had 'celiac axis compression syndrome.' It's a very rare disorder involving the celiac artery, one found mostly in older people."

Kathy is from a Christian home, so her family and friends began to pray. They prayed for a miracle. She says, "I prayed for healing too. The Lord gave me peace about my sickness. I never doubted it came for some reason. While I never doubted,

I did wonder if I would ever find out that reason.

"Well, twenty years later I did. It came in the form of my nine-year-old daughter. She was ill, in severe pain, and had lost fifteen pounds in three weeks. Most likely she would not live too many more weeks. I was able to suggest to her doctors that she might have a rare disorder in her artery near her heart. And while they thought it would be highly unlikely—because it couldn't occur in a child—the doctors did look into it and found the same condition I had. But they had to admit it was something they never would have thought to look for. They had never heard of it! And although my daughter still deals with daily pain, she is with us and able to thrive. Now *she* wonders why the Lord let her go through this. But she also trusts the Lord's will."

Kathy's story is probably repeated a million times a day. Someone prays for something that God denies and then uses his "wrong answer" to accomplish something else—perhaps a generation or even generations later. The will of God plays out in many areas besides the physical. Kathy's great distinction is that she trusted from the beginning that God had a greater purpose whether or not she would ever recognize it.

While it's nice to hear that God's better will triumphs in cases of infertility, adoption and lifesaving medical diagnoses, most of us pray about more mundane matters like jobs, money, houses, school, church and friendships. That's the story of the Clark family as they contemplated a move back in 1976. They wavered between remodeling their old house or finding a new one. They shopped around and found a house they loved on a lakeside lot. The day they listed their old house for sale they made an offer on their "dream home," only to discover it had sold that morning. Disappointment turned to delight three weeks later when a newer house came on the market—same lake, $5,000 less. They bought it, moved in and decided that their new house was better than they could have hoped. Ann Clark adds an interesting epilogue to their story. The week after their "dream house" slipped through their hands she attended a neighborhood prayer group. The leader opened by going around the circle to share an answer to prayer that people had recently experienced. "When I shared that God had answered my prayer with a *no*," Ann says, "I got a rather chilly response. We didn't know then what the future held. But apparently they weren't real familiar with God saying *no*."

Too Small to See

Ruth Graham adds her perspective to unanswered prayers in a personal story:

> He was not quite tall enough to see over the dashboard of the car I was driving.
>
> "Hurry up, Mom!" he urged.
>
> But he was too young to read the road signs that said forty-five miles per hour. As I began to apply the brakes, he demanded, "Why are you stopping?"
>
> "There is a school bus that has just stopped," I explained.
>
> I thought to myself, "How like me when I pray." Spiritually I am too young to read the road signs, too small to see what lies ahead. Yet, how often I am guilty of telling God how to run things.
>
> We may make our requests, but never insist on having our own way lest we become one of those of whom it was said, "He gave them their request; but sent leanness into their soul" (Psalm 106:15).
>
> We may pray in simple, childlike faith urgently, persistently. But we must always pray, "Thy will be done."[2]

Prayer always requires faith—faith in the existence of God, the hearing of God, the power of God, the goodness of God and the answer of God. Ruth Graham calls us to faith in the sovereignty of God. God knows what we do not know. God sees what we do not see. Every time we pray our requests and incorporate "thy will be done" we are not abdicating faith or excusing God for possible non-answers. To the contrary, we are acknowledging that we are mortal humans limited by size, knowledge and sinfulness. Like a child, we are free to speak our minds and hearts. Like a child, we are grateful for a Parent who knows better and places higher limits on our lesser requests.

When Jesus' Will Was Different

Jesus faced the same prayer problem we face. Even though he was and is fully God, he was still capable of praying prayers contrary to and subject to the will of God the Father. It's one of the most amazing insights we have into the life of Jesus and his relationship with the Father.

The night before Jesus was crucified he knew what was coming. For any of us to face death is hard enough, but Jesus' circumstances were unique. Only rarely does anyone know when and how he will die. As much as we might say we would like advance warning, we really prefer to face death by surprise. Jesus knew that his time was less than twenty-four hours away.

Death by crucifixion is a tortuous way to die. The Romans used this form of capital punishment as a deterrent to crime, nailing men to crosses placed along public thoroughfares. Death came slowly, often after many days. Blood loss wasn't enough to end a life. The ultimate cause of death was usually exposure, thirst or asphyxiation. It took an intense effort for the victim to breathe, heaving up and down on the cross in order to inhale and exhale. As if all of this wasn't agony enough, those crucified were further humiliated by total nakedness and the verbal taunts of observers.

Jesus was as human as we are—it is no wonder he didn't want to be crucified. He was also fully divine. As the Son of God he had existed forever. Death was alien to who he was, the farthest event from deity. But the greatest horror was—as God-Man—to have human sin transferred to him at the crucifixion. "God made him who had no sin to be sin for us" (2 Corinthians 5:21). Sin was absolutely repulsive to Jesus, yet he bore our sins on the Cross.

As his crucifixion day drew closer Jesus wanted to be alone. He wanted to pray. His prayer was for the love and strength he knew the Father would give to him. His prayer was for a way to sidestep the crucifixion. He went to one of his favorite places on the Mount of Olives, just east of Jerusalem.

> Then Jesus went with his disciples to a place called Gethsemane, and he said to them, "Sit here while I go over there and pray." He took Peter and the two sons of Zebedee along with him, and he began to be sorrowful and troubled. Then he said to them, "My soul is overwhelmed with sorrow to the point of death. Stay here and keep watch with me."
>
> Going a little farther, he fell with his face to the ground and prayed, "My Father, if it is possible, may this cup be taken from me. Yet not as I will, but as you will."
>
> Then he returned to his disciples and found them sleeping. "Could you men not keep watch with me for one hour?" he asked Peter. "Watch and pray so that you will not fall into temptation. The spirit is willing, but the body is weak."
>
> He went away a second time and prayed, "My Father, if it is not possible for this cup to be taken away unless I drink it, may your will be done."
>
> When he came back, he again found them sleeping, because their eyes were heavy. So he left them and went away once more and prayed the third time, saying the same thing.
>
> Matthew 26:36–44

To understand what happened here we need some background. The Son of God, theologians say, is *one* of *three* eternal Persons of the Trinity—"person" defined as possessing intellect, emotion and volition. So while the Trinity is *one* God, the Father, Son and Spirit, *each* has his own mind, feelings and will.

This helps explain why Jesus often said there were matters known to the Father but not to him—such as the exact timing of future events. When the Son became human in the person of Jesus, he gave up some of the independent use of his divine attributes—he became temporarily dependent on the Father and the Spirit for knowledge and power.

Jesus was still God, yet a separate person. He had a will of his own. The Father willed for Jesus to die on the cross. Jesus willed not to die. When the Father and Jesus looked into the future, they chose opposite courses of action. No doubt Jesus' humanity played a significant part in his desire to live.

When Jesus prayed in the Garden of Gethsemane he specifically asked the Father to find a way for him to avoid the crucifixion. He asked that he not have to drink this "cup" of death, that it be taken from him. Apparently Jesus knew what the Father willed on this matter—that the crucifixion go ahead as planned. Yet he still prayed for another way. The Father's answer was a compassionate but clear *no*. Because the Father loved the world he insisted that Jesus die (John 3:16).

Jesus did exactly what we do when we want something God doesn't want for us. He asked again—only the second time he "prayed more earnestly" (Luke 22:44). As Jesus asked God for this favor his passion was so great that "his sweat was like drops of blood falling to the ground" (Luke 22:44). There was no lack of faith. There was no problem with the Father-Son relationship. Jesus prayed as hard as he could. But the answer was still *no*.

Jesus didn't easily give up. He prayed again the same way with the same words. Like us, he hoped that persistence would change God's mind. Like us, he was reluctant to take no for an answer. Like us, he prayed the best he could to get what he wanted. But the answer didn't change.

Jesus no doubt in his mind understood what was best. He could grasp why the Father prodded him onward. So why did he disagree with God? Because our thinking and feeling and choosing aren't separated by sharp lines. Each part of us influences our other parts. A decision can't be purely intellectual any more than it can be wholly emotional. Even though Jesus knew intellectually that the purpose of his life was to die on the cross, his will still chose to live. Intellect doesn't rule the choices we make.

Most significant is that when Jesus' will clashed with the Father's will Jesus submitted, even though the disappointment and cost could not have been greater. In the end Jesus' choice was to obey his Father's will. He was convinced that his Father's choice would ultimately prove to be right.

Jesus was alone when God said *no* to his most passionate series of prayers. Yet the occasion and content of the prayers are reported multiple times in the New Testament. How did Jesus' biographers know about his confidential conversations with the Father? Jesus must have told them. And one of the reasons for telling was to help us when we pray.

From Jesus' example we learn some of prayer's most important lessons:

1. *Our personal desires that are contrary to God's will are not necessarily wrong.* Jesus didn't sin when he willed his own will and prayed for his way over the Father's way. God knows our individuality and acknowledges the independence of each human will. There is nothing wrong with wanting something different from what God wants for us.

2. *Our repeated requests are appropriate, even after God has said no.* In some cases God may change his *no* to *yes.* But even if God still says *no* he welcomes our continued communication. He will help us through the difficult process of disappointment. He understands when we want something so much that we are slow to take *no* for God's final answer.

3. *Our final purpose is to submit to God's will—whether we agree or not.* I don't sense that Jesus left the Garden that night fully persuaded. He was no more enthusiastic about being crucified when he left than when he came. It remained so hard for him, in fact, that he nearly died anticipating death! However, Jesus' greatest and final choice was to bend his will to conform with

the will of the Father. He chose to go along with what God wanted even though he didn't feel like it. That isn't easy in life's hardest times. It wasn't for Jesus and it won't be for us. As Christians, we make that ultimate choice by faith, convinced that God is right even if we can't see it or agree with it, having determined in advance to go along with God's will even when we would rather not. "Not my will, but yours be done" is our final prayer.

How Should We Pray?

How then should we pray? What should we do when God says *no* and his choice upsets or even grieves us?

Begin With the End

As much as possible, let us decide in advance to do what Jesus did and submit to God's will when we disagree.

For most of us that isn't a difficult decision to make—*in theory.* We believe God is wise and good and powerful. It makes sense to us that he knows better than we know and that his will is superior. Those who are reluctant to commit ahead of time to submission may fear God will somehow take advantage of them—telling them to do something they never would have agreed to had they known in advance. What if I promise ahead of time, for example, to bend my will to God's will and then find out that God expects me to become a missionary to some distant nation or that God wills for my beloved little girl to die a tragic, untimely death?

I don't have any words to make this easier. It eventually comes down to faith. Do I really trust God or not? Is he a good and loving God who will never cause me harm? When I am certain of those things I will agree in advance to whatever he chooses—even if I die without understanding the reasons for his choices.

So no matter what the outcome of my prayers, I have decided in advance to go with God's will. I can't foresee how circumstances will turn out, but I do know that God's will is my ultimate desire.

Seek God's Will

Instead of praying whatever comes to mind, let us try our best to determine God's will before we pray and then pray God's will back to him. This is our best opportunity to comply with 1 John 5:14: "This is the confidence we have in approaching God: that if we ask anything according to his will, he hears us."

That's easier to do than it might sound to you. The Bible is loaded with declarations of God's will:

1 Thessalonians 4:3: It is God's will that you should be sanctified: that you should avoid sexual immorality.

1 Thessalonians 5:18: Give thanks in all circumstances, for this is God's will for you in Christ Jesus.

1 Peter 2:15: For it is God's will that by doing good you should silence the ignorant talk of foolish men.

Ephesians 5:17–21: Therefore do not be foolish, but understand what the Lord's will is: Do not get drunk on wine, which leads to debauchery. Instead, be filled with the Spirit. Speak to one another with psalms, hymns and spiritual songs. Sing and make music in your heart to the Lord, always giving thanks to God the Father for everything, in the name of our Lord Jesus Christ. Submit to one another out of reverence for Christ.

These are only a few of the hundreds of the Bible's direct statements of God's will for our lives. God tells us that he wills for us to be saved, to be sanctified, not to marry non-Christians, to avoid lawsuits against believers and to tell the truth. For a high percentage of our daily lives God's will is already revealed to us.

The Bible's revelations focus primarily on how to live Christianly within the wide range of human experiences. The Bible doesn't give us specifics about God's will regarding which job offer to accept, which school to attend or which Christian man or woman to marry. Unfortunately, many of us agonize over the details we don't have and ignore the broad swath of information we do have. It's wise to assume that God has told us most of what we need to discern his will and that what he hasn't told us is comparatively less important.

It's our task to read the Bible, learn God's revealed will and then to pray according to that will in full expectation that God will answer *yes* to such prayers. In cases where the Bible doesn't reveal God's specific will we have several alternatives:

1. *Ask God for wisdom about his will.* James 1:5 says that "if any of you lacks wisdom, he should ask God, who gives generously to all without finding fault, and it will be given to him." In other words, our first prayer should be for *insight* into God's will so that we will be guided by the Spirit into *prayer* according to God's will.

2. *Assume that God gives freedom in this matter.* When God doesn't make his will known to us—and what he wants can't be deduced from other biblical principles—it may be that he allows us to choose either way. When we pray it is helpful to acknowledge to ourselves and God that this is our approach. You might pray along these lines: *Lord, I haven't been able to figure out your will in this matter. I'm assuming that I have the freedom to choose for myself between leasing the apartment on the fourth floor and leasing the apartment on the seventh floor. So I'm asking you to help me get the seventh floor apartment. I ask for your help to meet the right neighbors and to use this apartment in a way that will glorify you. If I'm misunderstanding your mind on this, please make that clear to me.*

3. *Admit that you haven't been able to determine God's will and turn the prayer over to the Holy Spirit to pray.* Hard as we try, sometimes we aren't able to know God's will. God may have kept his will a secret or our tack may be wrong. Whatever the rea-

son, when we don't know how to pray we ask the Holy Spirit to pray our prayers for us. Romans 8:26–27 says that "the Spirit helps us in our weakness. We do not know what we ought to pray for, but the Spirit himself intercedes for us with groans that words cannot express. And he who searches our hearts knows the mind of the Spirit, because the Spirit intercedes for the saints in accordance with God's will."

Pray According to God's Will

When we struggle and find God's will we find increased opportunities to pray with confidence according to God's will. When we know God's will, in other words, we will pray it and obtain what we seek.

Acknowledge God's Will in All of Life's Plans

While the practice isn't as popular as it used to be, some Christians write "D.V." in their letters whenever they mention future plans. The author of a letter may write, "Thank you for the invitation to spend August 5–12 at your seashore cottage. I am looking forward to spending a wonderful week together with you and with your family. D.V." The letters at the end are an abbreviation for the Latin *Deus Volit* (God willing). The practice grows out of James 4:13–15:

> Now listen, you who say, "Today or tomorrow we will go to this or that city, spend a year there, carry on business and make money."
> Why, you do not even know what will happen tomorrow. What is your life? You are a mist that appears for a little while and then vanishes.
> Instead, you ought to say, "If it is the Lord's will, we will live and do this or that."

The principle is more important than some legalistic practice. As Christians we are to live with a pervasive sense of God's will prevailing over our plans. We believe that God is sovereign and that in everything we are subject to his will.

Praying God's Will

Sovereign Lord, you created me with a will of my own and you know that it can be very strong. I make up my mind what I want and the way I want it. I am so sure that I am right and I try to convince you to make my will happen.

In my mind, I know that your will is far better than mine. In my heart I want your will in everything.

My problem is that my will too often gets in the way of your will. I fail to seek your will in all that I do. Many times I am blind and deaf to what you have so clearly revealed.

Honestly, my will won't go away. Since you created me this way I'll always have this strong will of my own. Today I will to choose your will. My heart's desire is to submit to you. With your help I will seek your thoughts and think them after you. I will obey your will even if it means surrendering what I really want.

Whatever the decision . . . not as I will, but as you will. Amen.

Notes

1. Emphasis added.
2. Ruth Graham, "By the Way," *Christianity Today* (September 4, 1981), p. 35.

SEVEN

The Time Isn't Right

There is a time for everything,
and a season for every activity under heaven:
a time to be born and a time to die,
a time to plant and a time to uproot,
a time to kill and a time to heal,
a time to tear down and a time to build,
a time to weep and a time to laugh,
a time to mourn and a time to dance,
a time to scatter stones and a time to gather them,
a time to embrace and a time to refrain,
a time to search and a time to give up,
a time to keep and a time to throw away,
a time to tear and a time to mend,
a time to be silent and a time to speak,
a time to love and a time to hate,
a time for war and a time for peace.

Ecclesiastes 3:1–8

We live in a world of clocks. Time is important. We are constantly measuring. Waiting. Foot-tapping and finger-drumming. One of the first questions of every patient with a terminal disease is, "How much time do I have?" Every child grows up hearing, "Not now, wait until you're older!" I can remember being a teenager with exactly a thousand days to wait before I could get a driver's permit.

The power of time significantly affects our understanding of unanswered prayer. Often God responds to our pleas with *no—for now*. It isn't that he has rejected our requests but deferred the answer until later. Just like the child who jumps to the conclusion that his mom and dad's "we'll see" always means "no—not ever," we assume that God's "wait for a while" means "wait forever."

Jesus by the Clock

Jesus frequently answered questions and requests with "later":

"My time has not yet come" (John 2:4).

"The right time for me has not yet come" (John 7:6).

"His time had not yet come" (John 7:30; 8:20).

Even in urgent situations Jesus didn't seem rushed. One day a man named Jairus came to Jesus with an urgent prayer for his dying daughter. He fell at Jesus' feet and prayed to him, asking him to come and heal her before she died. Jesus started in the direction of Jairus' home but was delayed by the crush of the crowd. In that crowd was a woman who also was ill, with a twelve-year hemorrhage. She touched Jesus and was healed in an instant, though we can assume she had prayed—and waited—for that healing for a dozen years. While Jesus was talking with her a message arrived that Jairus' daughter had died. It was too late. "Don't bother the teacher any more," the messenger told Jairus (Luke 8:49). But Jesus ran on a different clock. He continued to the girl's house, raised her up and she was well. He answered Jairus' prayer in a way that left him and his wife astonished—the timing wasn't what they expected but the prayer was answered *yes*.

Jesus' most painful delay was his belated visit to his sick friend Lazarus. Lazarus and his family were among Jesus' best friends. Jesus didn't delay because the relationship wasn't good—it was among the very best. But he showed up at least four days after his friend was dead and buried. Not exactly a quick answer to prayer. Jesus didn't delay because he didn't care—Jesus wept openly at Lazarus' tomb. Strangers were impressed enough to say, "See how he loved him!" (John 11:36). The only explanation Jesus gave for his long delay and the suffering of those he loved was "so that you may believe" (John 11:15).

Jesus demonstrated that there are many times when he hears prayers, loves the people praying, has every intention of granting their requests—and yet says *No . . . for now*. Obviously he doesn't always share our urgency. Although there are situations when Jesus impresses his urgency on us and we are the ones who are slow, for him it seems more important *what* is done than *when* it is done.

Surely one of the reasons the Bible gives us these examples is to help us understand and accept that later doesn't mean never. One vital component of our faith is a trust that God's timing is better than ours. God will take care of what seems urgent to us at a time and in a way he knows to be better.

This isn't an easy lesson to learn when we are frightened by our circumstances or suffering crushing pain in the present. Consider the situations of Job and Daniel.

Job's Waiting in Pain

I mentioned Job earlier—how calamity struck this man of unsurpassed riches, happiness and godliness. In a swift succession of disasters all ten of his children died, his great wealth was reduced to poverty and his good health turned into anguish. He was "ruined without any reason" (Job 2:3). What he didn't know was that his life was the field of competition between God and Satan, between good and evil. Ironically, he never did learn the reasons for his afflictions.

Yet the story that begins so tragically ends triumphantly. God eventually returned Job's health, multiplied his wealth and blessed him with ten more children. But the wait wasn't easy. During the interim Job's suffering was so intense that his prayers were suicidal:

> If only my anguish could be weighed and all my misery be placed on the scales! It surely would outweigh the sand of the seas—
> Oh, that I might have my request, that God would grant what I hope for, that God would be willing to crush me, to let loose his hand and cut me off!
>
> Job 6:2–3; 8–9

One of Job's hospital visitors was his friend Eliphaz, who gave Job advice on how to pray under such conditions:

> If it were I, I would appeal to God; I would lay my cause before him.
> He performs wonders that cannot be fathomed, miracles that cannot be counted.
>
> Job 5:8–9

Eliphaz was right. Those who suffer should appeal to God, who indeed answers prayer and performs miracles. What Eliphaz didn't take into consideration was God's timeline—what we could call the "divine delay." When God didn't answer with an immediate *yes*, Eliphaz assumed something was wrong with Job or with his prayers. That was Eliphaz' mistake.

Amid his suffering Job prayed contradictory prayers—some for health, some for death. God couldn't give both. And God wouldn't give death. In his severe pain Job had lost perspective of God's grander scheme. To Job the big issues were the taste-lessness of food and his loss of appetite (Job 6:6–7) and trying to get to sleep at night (Job 7:4). He needed God to filter out his inappropriate and irrational prayers, answering them with *no*. He needed God's stable wisdom to decide which prayers to grant and when to grant them.

It's easy to be an Eliphaz who rationalizes and spiritualizes away another's pain. It's quite another matter to be a Job—the one who suffers constant anguish, the one who has to wait for God. For the sufferer and those who truly suffer alongside the sufferer, waiting can be faith's greatest test. To wait for God's remedy when every second is painful can be indescribably hard.

Daniel and the Delayed Angel

Daniel was one of the greatest and godliest men who ever lived. His biography is filled with supernatural events: surviving a fiery furnace, living in a lion's den, receiving protection against evil enemies and rising to high positions of political power. More than anything else, Daniel was a man of prayer. He prayed even when a death sentence hung over him for continuing in his habit of praying to the one true God. All the power of a world empire couldn't shut him up. Yet even Daniel had to wait for an answer to one of his most passionate prayers.

It happened in Babylon back in the sixth century B.C., toward the end of Daniel's life. Far from the homeland of his Jewish heritage, Daniel had a disturbing vision of the future. As he sought God's help in understanding the political conflicts that had left Israel in national captivity he didn't just pray—he fasted from good food, ate no meat, drank no wine and surrendered personal comforts for three weeks. Finally, an angel showed up with an answer from God. Here is what the angel said:

> Do not be afraid, Daniel. Since the first day that you

set your mind to gain understanding and to humble yourself before your God, your words were heard, and I have
come in response to them. But the prince of the Persian
kingdom resisted me twenty-one days. Then Michael,
one of the chief princes, came to help me, because I was
detained there with the king of Persia. Now I have come
to explain to you what will happen to your people in the
future, for the vision concerns a time not yet come.

Daniel 10:12–14

Within this angelic speech there are some remarkable insights into unanswered prayer:

Daniel's prayer was instantly answered by God in heaven.

God's answer took three weeks to get from God to Daniel,
even though it was sent via an angel.

There were powerful forces of evil—in this case a demon
called "the prince of the Persian kingdom"—opposing God's
answer to Daniel's prayer.

Daniel didn't know the reason for the delay, although the
delay was valid.

The message from the angel included an announcement of
further delays before the answers to Daniel's prayers would be
fully implemented.

We can't take this to mean that every delayed or unanswered prayer has been slowed by the spiritual battles of angels
and demons. The point is that godly saints who pray worthy
prayers God is happy to grant don't always get the instant answers they want. Prayer enters the ultimate realms of spiritual
conflict between good and evil. The fact that we usually can't
see the conflict makes it no less fierce. Our ignorance doesn't
make the warfare less real. And the situation hasn't changed
since the time of Daniel. Even now our struggle "is not against
flesh and blood, but against the rulers, against the authorities,
against the powers of this dark world and against the spiritual
forces of evil in the heavenly realms" (Ephesians 6:12). This
couldn't be more serious. This spiritual war requires supernatural powers and weapons. It is as foolish to think that we can

win against demons as it is to try to fight off nuclear weapons with baseball bats.

The enormity of the conflict and the delays our prayers may encounter aren't reasons to be pessimistic. In the long run we will win. We have the power of God, which bests the power of demons. Because we "are from God and . . . because the one who is in you is greater than the one who is in the world" (1 John 4:4), we are guaranteed final victory. Until that final victory is ours we are to engage in spiritual warfare with weapons adequate for the fight:

> Therefore put on the full armor of God, so that when the day of evil comes, you may be able to stand your ground, and after you have done everything, to stand.
>
> Stand firm then, with the belt of truth buckled around your waist, with the breastplate of righteousness in place, and with your feet fitted with the readiness that comes from the gospel of peace.
>
> In addition to all this, take up the shield of faith, with which you can extinguish all the flaming arrows of the evil one.
>
> Take the helmet of salvation and the sword of the Spirit, which is the word of God.
>
> *And pray in the Spirit on all occasions with all kinds of prayers and requests. With this in mind, be alert and always keep on praying for all the saints.*[1]
>
> Ephesians 6:13–18

The Schedule of God

God hears billions of prayers and answers them according to his will and for our good. The complexity of how he brings together the details of all people, all prayers and all circumstances is infinitely mind-stretching. It requires that pieces fall into place in a sequence only God can fathom. For instance:

A woman prays for years to be married to the right man. God has chosen someone for her who is already married but whose wife will someday die. God's answer to her prayer depends on a circumstance unknown to her that may take years to play out.

The chronically ill patient needs an organ transplant that requires the death of a person whose time hasn't yet come. A difficult delay for one is a delightful delay for the other. God coordinates the two.

A teenager prays to God for information about the cause of her grandmother's death. The answer is a genetic disorder unknowingly inherited by the teen who prayed. God postpones the answer because the knowledge will do her no good. The Lord may give the answer forty years later when a breakthrough gene therapy can make a difference in her life.

All of this returns again to the central issue of unanswered prayer—trusting God. When we see no answer or God's answer is *no* we must choose whether or not we will trust God—even when we don't understand or want to accept his response. Trust requires us as Christians to believe God is right, whether we agree or not. It's the confidence of Romans 8:26–31:

> The Spirit helps us in our weakness. We do not know what we ought to pray for, but the Spirit himself intercedes for us with groans that words cannot express. And he who searches our hearts knows the mind of the Spirit, because the Spirit intercedes for the saints in accordance with God's will. *And we know that in all things God works for the good of those who love him, who have been called according to his purpose.*
>
> For those God foreknew he also predestined to be conformed to the likeness of his Son, that he might be the firstborn among many brothers. And those he predestined, he also called; those he called, he also justified; those he justified, he also glorified.
>
> *What, then, shall we say in response to this? If God is for us, who can be against us?*[2]

What If We Die Before the Answer Comes?

David proclaimed that "I am still confident of this: I will see the goodness of the LORD in the land of the living" (Psalm 27:13). We will certainly see God's uncountable blessings in this "land of the living." But are we guaranteed in-our-lifetime delivery on any and all of our prayers? Real life tells us that sometimes our problems outlive us. Our lives wind down before our prayers are answered. Why? What does it say about God and prayer if we die before God's answer arrives? Just how long does God expect us to wait for him?

Esther was a devout Christian, the organist for many years in her Swedish Lutheran Church. The attitudes and behavior of her son-in-law, Tom, greatly concerned her. Whenever anyone talked to Tom about Christian ideals or anything related to church or God, he answered, "Who can believe that rubbish anyway? That Christian stuff is nothing but garbage!" Esther prayed for twenty-five years that her son-in-law would become a Christian. She died without seeing any change—even a small sign of hope.

A few years after Esther's death Tom and his wife, Shirley, moved to a new country home. Shirley followed her mother's example and found a church home in a small town nearby. Because Tom didn't like staying home alone he started to go along with his wife to the church services. To everyone's amazement—including Tom's—he liked it! He especially liked the pastor and even bragged to others about his sermons. Within a few months he changed from a skeptic to a believer. Tom joined the church, became an usher, volunteers for the church food shelf and started teaching a course on Jewish history. It wasn't a brief aberration. Tom didn't go back to his disbelief. He continues those ministries today.

Many may wonder if Esther, in heaven, knows what happened to Tom on earth. Whether or not she knows, her long-time prayers were answered. Even if she didn't live to see the results, God proved faithful.

For twenty-two years Dr. Arthur Lewis taught New Testament at Bethel College in Arden Hills, Minnesota. Some time after he retired in 1988, he suffered a stroke that took away his ability to walk and the use of his left (strong) hand. In an essay titled "Will This Suffering Ever End?"[3] Lewis offers a personal look at Jesus' promise that "if you believe, you will receive whatever you ask for in prayer" (Matthew 21:22). He writes that "for the first time I can empathize with believers whose prayers about suffering are not answered. I have had time to reconsider the biblical promises regarding prayer, and I discovered I overlooked something." He then explains that "God will indeed give us whatever we ask, but not necessarily right away or at the time we want it." Many of our prayers, Lewis says, will be answered not in this present time but in eternity. He bases his understanding on the words of Jesus in John 16:23: "In that day you will no longer ask me anything. I tell you the truth, my Father will give you whatever you ask in my name." The expression "that day" refers to the *eschaton*, or end times—not just the future on earth but the future in heaven as well.

Lewis details three promises for the future:

1. *The resurrection of our bodies.* Every Christian can anticipate a resurrection life and a resurrection body like the body of Jesus (see John 11:24 and 1 Corinthians 15:51–52). Most of us will receive this gift after we have been dead and buried, although Christians alive at the time of Jesus' return will go from this life and body to the resurrection life and body without passing through death.

According to Lewis, "when we ask God for the miracle of healing or pray for sick loved ones, we have no assurance that our prayers will be answered at this time, but we can be assured that He will restore our physical bodies to perfect health at His second coming 'when the dead shall be raised imperishable.' "

2. *A new earth as our dwelling.* Sin has marred not only humans but all of creation. Jesus' redemption includes not only sinners but the earth as well. Paul explains "that the creation

itself will be liberated from its bondage to decay and brought into the glorious freedom of the children of God. We know that the whole creation has been groaning as in the pains of childbirth right up to the present time" (Romans 8:21–22). In other words, the world is waiting to get past the pain of sin and its consequences and back to the way God really intended creation to be.

When this happens God will be with them (all of us saints who have suffered) and "wipe away every tear from their eyes. There will be no more death or mourning or crying or pain, for the old order of things has passed away" (Revelation 21:4). That will be great! The prayers of suffering people throughout history will be wonderfully answered by God.

3. *The defeat of God's enemies.* Based on Psalm 110:1, 1 Corinthians 15:25 and Philippians 3:21, Lewis looks forward to the final victory over Satan, demons and evil. Every enemy of God, righteousness and believers will be permanently defeated.

Combining the scholarship of a New Testament professor and the experience of a man suffering from the after effects of a stroke, Lewis concludes that "these three promises give us hope of great joy at His coming (John 16:22), and of receiving God's answers to all of our prayers (John 16:23). But while we wait we have also been promised 'sufficient grace' (2 Corinthians 12:9) to enable us to hang on. Jesus also said He would send the Comforter to be with us (John 16:7, KJV). I believe I can wait until His coming for the answer to my prayers. What about you?"

Patience and Trust

I'm not always sure about me, Lord. I have my doubts. I always seem to be in a hurry. When I pray I want your answer not only my way but in my time. I can get discouraged thinking that today's prayer might not be answered for three weeks, or for three hundred years. I'm just not sure how long I can wait.

And I'm really not sure about others. By comparison, my situation is safe and comfortable. But what about those who have chronic pain? What about the desperately lonely? What about the people who are so very poor? If I had a choice I guess I would rather that you give them what they ask now and let me wait until much later. My pains seem few; my possessions are many; my questions can wait.

No, I'm not sure about me.

But I am sure about you. I truly believe you know what you are doing. You are wise beyond my understanding. Your clock ticks out a thousand years to my minute or a minute to my thousand years. You not only have everything figured out, you have everything planned out. Your plans for us are to do good, not harm. You know exactly when we should hear your answers and exactly when we should receive your answers.

My problem is reconciling my impatience with your providence. Please teach me. Encourage me. Make me patient. Give me that sufficient grace you promised.

I'm looking forward to when all our prayers are answered! Until then, I'll trust you 100 percent. Amen.

Notes

1. Emphasis added.
2. Emphasis added.
3. Arthur Lewis, "Will This Suffering Ever End?", *the standard* (August/September 1994), pp. 21–22.

EIGHT

Something Else May Be More Important

On November 22, 1963, John F. Kennedy was assassinated. During the weeks before that unexpected attack one of the senior editors of the *Chicago Sun-Times* graciously showed interest in me and my journalism. I was a college student, the editor of our campus newspaper. He offered to give me and other members of the student newspaper staff a tour of the *Sun-Times* editorial offices.

The day after the assassination America was shocked into mourning. Uncertainty and fear gripped the nation. Businesses closed. College classes were canceled.

Since I had an unexpected day off school I called the newspaper editor and asked him if that day would be okay for my colleagues and me to tour his office. His answer was short and to the point. He said that he and his staff were exceptionally busy. He said not to come.

At the time I was offended. Now I understand that my request was absurdly inappropriate. I was interrupting him in the middle one of the busiest news days in the history of American journalism. Rumors were rampant. News stories broke by the minute. Extra editions kept the presses running around the clock. There were far more important things to do than give office tours to teenage college students who didn't realize they were witnessing some of the most significant events in history.

What I thought at the time was a valid request I now realize was embarrassingly inappropriate.

God must often hear prayers like that from me. At the time it seems like a great idea to ask him for health, wealth, possessions, relationships and information. When God says *no* I am tempted to be offended. Years later I gain a different perspective that shows God was right to decline my prayer.

The God of Priorities

Like us, God must order his priorities. He weighs what is more important and what is less important. As hard as it is for us to understand at the time, our requests may be far less important to God than they are to us.

That isn't to say that any one of us is unimportant to God. It isn't to say that God is unconcerned about our needs and desires. And it isn't to say that God doesn't hear or doesn't care when we plead with him. Rather, God must do what God must do. It is part of his divine nature and responsibility to prioritize and to bring about what he knows to be the greatest good—even if it conflicts with the prayers of those he loves.

In God's providence, he eventually works everything together for good (Romans 8:28). He grants requests when they are *best* answered—sooner for some, later for others. He teaches us that today's disappointment will make sense tomorrow. In everything he acts with a higher priority on achieving our good than on simply granting our prayers.

The Bible gives many examples.

Obedience Over Tears

> You came back and wept before the Lord, but he paid
> no attention to your weeping and turned a deaf ear to you.
>
> Deuteronomy 1:45

It's difficult to say no when those you love plead with tears. God loved the people of Israel. Yet he turned a deaf ear to their tears.

God had great dreams for his special people. He set them free from their national slavery in Egypt, miraculously leading them through the Red Sea and the Sinai Desert. God promised them a wonderful home in Canaan, along the eastern shore of the Mediterranean. It was a land inhabited by strong peoples with walled cities. To conquer and occupy Canaan, Israel would need more miracles.

When the battle time came, Israel's army was too scared to attack. They lied to themselves that they would lose. The truth was that they were unwilling to trust God and to obey.

God was angry. He had done everything for them—miracle after miracle. He had proven he would give them every victory he promised. He had demonstrated that they would succeed every time they obeyed his orders. Nothing was convincing enough. In anger he announced that none of them would ever enter the Promised Land. God would wait an entire generation before giving a new home to the nation of Israel.

When the Israelites felt the heat of God's anger and heard the consequences of their disobedience they decided to go ahead and attack after all. Somehow they didn't realize that obedience a day late is actually disobedience. They were overwhelmingly defeated by the Amorites.

Now they were in a terrible spot. Behind them was a desert, a threat of death by time. In front of them were the Amorites, who had just demonstrated their military superiority. Above them was an angry God. They did what desperate people often do. They prayed. They confessed their sins. They wept with passion.

They wanted God to give them another chance. Now they were willing to fight, if only God would guarantee victory. God said *no*.

It's easy to misinterpret this story. God may seem unforgiving and unwilling to grant a second chance. We might conclude that if we don't do everything God's way he will strike and destroy us. God appears to be unfeeling and arbitrary.

The truth is that God loved these people. It must have caused him dire pain to say *no*. Every other evidence of God's character hints that God also cried when they wept. Like any father, he would have preferred to give them exactly what they wanted. They were hurting—and fathers love to heal the hurts of their children.

God had a higher priority. He wanted to teach Israel a powerful, permanent lesson: he was their king. He wanted to forever etch in their memory that his promises are always reliable, undeserving of doubts or second guesses. He wanted them to obey what he ordered, not play the part of God by denying or disobeying his orders. God concluded it was better for Israel to learn this painful lesson during forty years of wilderness waiting than to receive a quick answer to a teary prayer. The lesson would be hard but the benefits would last for generations.

To this day some wonder if God was not too harsh.

I believe God always does what is good for us, even if to us it seems harsh or too demanding. Like every loving parent he insists that his children learn to obey. Our obedience is more important in his view than our getting a *yes*, even to prayers wrapped in passion and tears.

God is fulfilling his great eternal purposes for history. Our requests impact not only our era but the whole future of the whole planet. God isn't willing to sacrifice future generations on the altar of an earlier generation's request. At times that means he will deny the prayers of the present.

How do we respond to this side of God? If we are the beneficiaries of others' lessons we should learn and celebrate.

That's one reason the Bible benefits us so much. Every story we read of the past teaches us how to live in the present. Every lesson we heed protects us from repeating the mistakes of others and preserves us from suffering their consequences. But what if we are the ones God is teaching? What if he denies our worried prayers as an example to others? Listen carefully, because this is an important truth to learn! There is great satisfaction in being the teaching tool of God. There is profound hope in knowing that God can use our loss for the ultimate gain of others—and that God can and will eventually bring us perfect good out of our present disappointment. Such faith can transform our lives. It's a confidence in a loving God who will do us no harm.

Peculiar circumstances had forced a surgeon to prepare to operate on his own son. Far from home with no other surgeons available, he knew his son would soon die without the operation. As the anesthesia was administered the little boy looked up at his physician father. "You won't hurt me, will you, Dad?" he asked. Fighting for control of his emotions, the surgeon gazed at his son. "Son," he spoke softly, "I may have to hurt you but I will never harm you."

At the time the son probably didn't understand the semantic difference between the words. Even so, the point was significant. The surgeon would have to cause his boy pain in order to help him. As a father, he wouldn't do anything to harm the son he loved.

God may say *no* to our prayers in spite of our pleading and crying. He may refuse to heed our requests. But he never stops loving and he will do us no harm. It takes faith to believe this perspective, of course, when circumstances indicate otherwise. When Job struggled to interpret his situation he accused God of not answering his prayers—and of actually attacking him:

> I cry out to you, O God, but you do not answer;
> I stand up but you merely look at me.
> You turn on me ruthlessly;

> with the might of your hand you attack me.
>
> Job 30:20–21

Job hadn't grasped the truth. Although God had allowed Satan to test Job for a time, God hadn't attacked Job. Although God didn't answer when and how Job asked, God wasn't unsympathetic. Eventually Job came to understand God's grace, but in the center of his pain his perspective overwhelmed his faith. It's wondrous that Job didn't give up on God even when God didn't answer his tearful pleas. When his wife counseled Job to "Curse God and die!" (Job 2:9) he remained faithful to God and sustained his integrity. It's quite amazing that Job could tell her, "You are talking like a foolish woman. Shall we accept good from God, and not trouble?" What a marvelous commendation that "In all this, Job did not sin in what he said" (Job 2:10).

This answer is easier for us to understand when life is going well but is most powerful when we share Job's misery. It's the lesson that God calls us to faithfulness and obedience even when we are oppressed and even when the outcome appears uncertain. It is all right to pray, to plead and to weep. But do not disobey. Let us allow God to choose what is most important.

Ascension Over Death

> Elijah was afraid and ran for his life. When he came to Beersheba in Judah, he left his servant there, while he himself went a day's journey into the desert. He came to a broom tree, sat down under it and prayed that he might die. "I have had enough, LORD," he said. "Take my life; I am no better than my ancestors."
>
> 1 Kings 19:3–4

People usually pray for life and are disappointed when God allows death. Elijah prayed for death and was disappointed when God allowed him to live.

Sometimes it can be appropriate to pray for death. I visited an elderly retired farmer in a nursing home. George told me that every morning he got up, knelt down next to his bed and prayed that God would let him die and go to heaven. His life had been long and full. Now he wanted to go to his new home in the presence of God. The Lord said *yes* to this prayer and I conducted his funeral.

Death isn't always the worst that can befall us. Martyred missionary Jim Elliot said that God is populating heaven and we dare not limit him to the very old. I have seen Christians behave unchristianly in the later decades of their lives, saying and doing things inconsistent with their lifelong values. Friends have prayed that they would die and go to be with God before they discredit his name and contradict what they have always believed.

Yes, it may be right to pray for death.

But it wasn't what God wanted when Elijah prayed to die. Elijah had just come off Mount Carmel and one of the greatest public displays of God's power in the entire Old Testament. He had stood alone against the pagan priests of Baal in a prayer battle. God had answered Elijah's prayers and proved that Baal was impotent and his prophets wrong. His victory further antagonized the wicked Queen Jezebel, who swore to assassinate him. Spiritually drained and physically exhausted, Elijah ran for his life and collapsed. He could see no better solution to his situation than death.

God said *no*. Instead of agreeing with Elijah's misguided prayer, God met Elijah's personal needs. An angel came to him, providing much needed sleep and food. But the reason God said *no* was far greater. God fully intended to bring Elijah to heaven, but not just now and not by means of death. God planned to miraculously translate Elijah from earth to heaven without dying. Without a doubt, it was a far better way to go!

As [Elijah and Elisha] were walking along and talking together, suddenly a chariot of fire and horses of fire ap-

peared and separated the two of them, and Elijah went up
to heaven in a whirlwind.

2 Kings 2:11

God often says *no* because he has something better planned
for those he loves. Our hearts can well up with thankfulness to
God that he knows what is better and more important. " 'For
I know the plans I have for you,' declares the LORD, 'plans to
prosper you and not to harm you, plans to give you hope and
a future' " (Jeremiah 29:11).

Divine Commitments Over Mother's Desires

The mother of Zebedee's sons came to Jesus with her
sons and, kneeling down, asked a favor of him.

"What is it you want?" he asked.

She said, "Grant that one of these two sons of mine
may sit at your right and the other at your left in your
kingdom."

"You don't know what you are asking," Jesus said to
them. "Can you drink the cup I am going to drink?"

"We can," they answered.

Jesus said to them, "You will indeed drink from my
cup, but to sit at my right or left is not for me to grant.
These places belong to those for whom they have been
prepared by my Father."

Matthew 20:20–24

For two thousand years Mrs. Zebedee has been unjustly denounced for her prayer. The criticism started immediately. The
other ten disciples of Jesus were perturbed that James and
John—the sons of Zebedee—wanted heaven's best seats. Their
mother has been condemned for everything from tactlessness
to greed for requesting the best spots for her boys.

But what's wrong with any mother praying for her children
to be as close to Jesus as possible? Shouldn't she be commended
for desiring the best for her sons? I love her prayer. She should

be a model for every Christian mother. Imagine what good could come from modern moms going straight to Jesus and asking that their sons and daughters be as close as possible to the Lord.

It was a wonderful prayer, but the answer was *no*. Not because Jesus didn't honor the woman. Not because he didn't want James and John forever close by his side. Multiple references throughout the Gospels indicate concentric circles around Jesus. There were thousands in the crowds who listened to him. About 120 composed the larger group of disciples (Acts 1:15). The twelve made up the smaller group of apostles. Three men—Peter, James and John—were in the inner circle present for special occasions and closest contact (Matthew 17:1; Mark 5:37). And John was Jesus' best friend (John 13:23; 21:7, 20). If Jesus ever kept a list of candidates for the seats closest to him in heaven, James and John would be at the top.

But the answer was still *no*. God the Father had already made plans for those seats. They were specially prepared. Who would occupy them had already been decided. When God makes a commitment he does it knowing all future contingencies and considerations. God keeps his commitments. He can't be prayed out of them—not even by a godly, well-meaning mother. Divine plans are more important than any mother's dreams.

Mrs. Zebedee probably was disappointed, but she need not have been:

The motive for her prayer was good.

The results were good, even if the answer was *no*. Her sons would be in heaven with Jesus and they were counted already in Jesus' inner circle. Mrs. Zebedee might not have gotten exactly what she requested, but what she got was great.

The knowledge that God keeps his commitments is a wonderful comfort. If persuasive mothers could pray God out of what he had already set his mind to do, any of us might be displaced from God's plans by somebody else's prayer.

Humility Over Healing

> To keep me from becoming conceited because of these surpassingly great revelations, there was given to me a thorn in the flesh, a messenger from Satan, to torment me. Three times I pleaded with the Lord to take it away from me. But he said to me, "My grace is sufficient for you, for my power is made perfect in weakness." Therefore I will boast all the more gladly about my weaknesses, so that Christ's power may rest on me. That is why, for Christ's sake, I delight in weaknesses, in insults, in hardships, in persecutions, in difficulties. For when I am weak, then I am strong.
>
> 2 Corinthians 12:7–10

God said *no* to Paul's prayer for healing. The Lord told him it was more important for him to be humble than to be healed. Humility is very important to God.

> All of you, clothe yourselves with humility toward one another, because, "God opposes the proud but gives grace to the humble." Humble yourselves, therefore, under God's mighty hand, that he may lift you up in due time.
>
> 1 Peter 5:5–6

Earlier in 2 Corinthians 12, Paul boasted about his spiritual experiences. Into his boasting he wove a story about a man who was given a preview of heaven and lived to tell about it. What this man saw was so spectacular that human vocabulary is insufficient to describe it. Many students of the Bible think Paul was in a roundabout way sharing his own experience—that maybe he died, went to heaven and was miraculously returned to this life by God. Whatever happened, Paul knew that the experience was so unusual and so impressive that he was likely to be overwhelmed by pride.

Against this backdrop of boasting Paul tells about his "thorn in the flesh." Whatever afflicted Paul, to him it was a serious problem. So he did what every Christian should do—

he prayed. He asked God to heal him. Like Jesus in the Garden of Gethsemane, Paul prayed three times. Three times he was told *no*.

With the divine no came a divine explanation, something we don't always receive. But God explained to Paul that allowing the thorn to continue to hurt him would keep him humble. In other words, the Lord knew that if the man who saw heaven had perfect health he would likely become proud. Unbearable. Unfit for ministry. The best solution was to leave him sick and humble rather than healthy and proud. We may wonder why God couldn't make him healthy and humble at the same time. That isn't explained to us.

I am thoroughly impressed with Paul's response. Many of us turn God's *no* into an excuse for resentment and bitterness or a reason to renounce faith and reject God. Paul took God's *no* as an opportunity for growth and teaching. The spiritual principle is that God's strength is often best demonstrated in human weakness. What does it prove about God if a person who is healthy, wealthy and strong lives Christianly? Anyone who has everything doesn't really need God. On the other hand, the very best place for God to show his greatness may be in a person who is weak and sick and struggling. If a person loves God and lives for God when life is hard, then God must really be worth loving and living for. Paul concluded that God could best be seen when Paul was weak. A strong, proud and boastful Paul would block out God.

Now we have to decide how this spiritual principle applies to each one of us. Would we rather have our prayers unanswered so we could be humble and pleasing to God? Are we willing to have a good attitude when God for our own good says *no?* Most of us prefer to say, "Come on, God, give me a try. Give me what I want and I promise to be the humblest person around." God knows us better than we know ourselves. He wants us to be like Jesus "who, being in very nature God . . . made himself nothing . . . he humbled himself and became obedient to death—even death on a cross!" (Philippians 2:6–

8). Humility is so important to God he is willing to do whatever it takes to make us like Jesus.

What Greater Good Does God Seek?

It wasn't easy for the Israelites, Elijah, Mrs. Zebedee and Paul to be told their prayers were less important than they thought. If they were anything like us they had a hard time accepting God's perception of their situation. We want God to think that we are the most important person he could ever hear, that our prayers warrant immediate attention and that what we want is flawlessly good. We word our prayers to persuade God that we are right and that he should grant whatever we want. It can feel degrading when God has other plans involving other people whom he says come first. "I'm going to give you something you need—but it's something you *don't* want," he says. "It's more important than what you think you need and what you *do* want."

When God says *no*, ask him what greater good he seeks. Not that you shouldn't ask again. Like Paul, go ahead and ask three times. Ask even more than three times. But between requests tell God that you trust him to prioritize—and that you are willing to take a lower number and wait. Tell him you trust him to make the best choice, even if to you it seems like the hard choice. It may be the hardest prayer you ever prayed. And perhaps the best and most important.

———

God of Israel, Elijah, John and James' mother, and of Paul, here is my request again. You've heard it before. You know every word I'm going to say. You know what I want before I ask. But I'm asking again.

What I want may not be as important to you as it is to me. That's hard for me to understand and accept.

As best I can, I submit to your priorities. I am convinced that you will do what is most important even if I must wait for what I want or take a permanent no.

Lord, when you tell me no, what are you after? What is the greater good you are trying to accomplish? Please give me eyes to see what you see. Help me to desire what you desire. Teach me to pray for those things that are highest on your list.

I really want to have the humble attitude and life of Jesus. I pray for that Christlikeness in Jesus' name. Amen.

NINE

Reasons for Prayers May Be Wrong

> *You do not have, because you do not ask God. When you ask, you do not receive, because you ask with wrong motives, that you may spend what you get on your pleasures.*
>
> James 4:2–3

Not long ago I received more than a dozen phone calls to my office in one week from a man whose name I didn't recognize. Every time he phoned I was unavailable to take the call. Each time he left his name but refused to give a number for me to call back. He wouldn't talk with anyone else in the office or even say why he was calling.

Concerned that the matter must be urgent, I left instructions that the next time he called I was to be interrupted—no matter what meeting or activity I was in. When I finally talked to him he told me he was soliciting advertising for the annual magazine of an organization I had never heard of. I explained that we do almost no such advertising and that those decisions are made by the business office, not by me. When I offered to transfer his call to the business department he said he preferred I make a personal donation to his organization and recommended a $35 cash gift. In return he promised to send to me a silver sticker.

When I finally convinced this man to talk to the business office, I put his call on hold. Intending to first explain all of this to the business manager, I mistakenly forwarded the call directly to the business office, so that the business manager received the call without any explanation. Not remembering which line the call came in on, I looked with bewilderment at a phone with fourteen outside lines flashing. One by one I picked up every line in an attempt to reconnect to the caller. I never found him—though I did cause a further mess by somehow causing all fourteen waiting lines to ring back to my desk.

It was a communication disaster, although it helped me understand what James 4:3 says about prayer: "When you ask, you do not receive, because you ask with wrong motives, that you may spend what you get on your pleasures." The man who called me didn't get what he wanted, and one of the reasons was that he didn't know how to ask. He gave little consideration to me as the giver; he seemed primarily concerned about his needs and interests as the receiver. The same thing happens when many Christians pray. We burst into God's presence, blurt our request at him and before long find we don't receive what we want. Wanting us to get our prayers answered, James and other authors of Scripture explain how wrong motives can be at the root of unanswered prayer.

Prayer Must Be Asked

James begins at the beginning of prayer. Before touching on motive he reminds us of something we probably already know: prayer must be *asked*. That should be obvious, but sometimes we miss the obvious.

James 4:2 warns that "You do not have, because you do not ask God." James means something broader than imploring God to give us what we want. He includes inviting God to involve himself in every part of our lives.

Compare it to asking a banker to lend you a million dollars for your business. The banker wants to meet you personally, see your books, visit your warehouse, interview your managers and learn as much as possible about your operation. It's impossible to isolate the million dollars you want from the banker's thoroughgoing involvement in your business and life. In fact, there is a business adage that says, "Make sure you borrow enough from the bank that the bank becomes more than your lender. If the loan is large the bank becomes your partner." When God hears our requests he doesn't isolate them from the rest of our lives. If he's going to answer our prayers God wants to be even more than our partner. He expects to be the Chief Executive Officer of our lives.

Proper prayer happens in a context of total life-sharing with God. I have an expression I often say to my wife, Charleen. It's a part of our marriage communication that may not make total sense to you, but it's meaningful to us. I talk to her about almost everything that goes on in my life—from major decisions to daily trivia. I share my dreams and ideas, my problems and concerns. And then I often say that "nothing seems real until I tell you about it." It's because she is such an important part of my life.

God intends the same sense of reality and closeness to happen through prayer. God is so vital to our lives that we should talk to him about everything—ask his opinions, his counsel and his will. It's as if "nothing is real" in our lives until we have first prayed about it to God.

It is in the backdrop of this constant communication with God that James 4:3 begins with "When you ask. . . ." For our prayer motives to be right, they should flow out of a relationship with God that overflows with communication—one in which we talk about and ask about nearly everything in our lives. Here's another way of saying this: asking is good and necessary, but every request is to be a part of daily dialogue with God about all of life.

Asking Doesn't Guarantee Receiving

One more time the Bible reminds us that asking doesn't guarantee receiving. James describes a common reality in prayer: "When you ask, *you do not receive*. . . ."[1] Answers to prayer are up to God, not us. God often turns down prayers or leaves them unanswered because they are based on improper motives. But even good motives are no guarantee of a *yes*. Bad motives can block God's answers. Good motives don't necessarily comply with God's will.

Sometimes wonderful Christians find themselves in difficult situations and pray as if this weren't true. They are convinced God will answer every prayer just as they request—if only they could get their prayers exactly right. They assume that the vastness of their faith is what provokes God's positive response. They assume that the more people they gather to pray the more likely they are to get the answer they want. Some even assume that loud, intense prayers assure right results.

God chooses how he will answer prayer. Let us never reduce him to a computer that will do what we ask because we punch in the right formula. God is a person, not a machine. The final decision is his, not ours. Faith is the belief he will do what is right and best, not that we will get the answer we want. Nevertheless, James 4:3 points out that part of prayer *is* dependent on us: prayers aren't answered because they are asked with wrong motives.

Motives Matter

Motives matter much of the time, but not always. Suppose you have a natural gas leak in your home. You could invite me over to help knowing that I really care about you and really want to fix the leak for you. I start out by lighting a match to determine where the leak is coming from. Your house blows up and you and I are seriously injured. Consider this: natural gas doesn't choose to explode or not explode based on my motives. In this case it doesn't matter whether I am motivated by love, stupidity or arson. The results are the same.

Where motives *always* matter is in relationships. If your next-door neighbor picks up your mail while you are away on vacation, you are happy or sad depending on your neighbor's motivation. You are glad if he aimed to help you. You are furious if he wanted to read your mail and invade your privacy.

Motives are crucial to prayer because prayer is totally based on the relationship between God and us. Relationships mean everything to God; they should matter very much to us. God highly values love, caring, forgiveness and commitment. He delights when we are on good terms with him and is deeply disappointed when we are on bad terms.

What all of this means is that God answers our prayers more on the basis of our relationship with him than on the depth of our desire to have our prayers answered. Compare it to human relationships—between co-workers, friends, lovers, parents and children, husbands and wives, employers and employees. When the relationship is good, we are much more likely to give what the other person asks. But when we know that the relationship is sour and the person is being selfish, we are likely to say no.

Imagine yourself on God's throne hearing the following requests. Decide for yourself which requests you would grant based on the underlying motives:

Request	Motive #1	Motive #2
Heal my illness	To prove God's greatness to unbelievers	To make me healthier than my brother
Make me rich	To help the poor	Because I like money
Call Jane to salvation	To save her soul	So I can marry her
Give wisdom to the president	Because 1 Tim. 2:1–2 commands us to pray for those in authority	Because he's a member of my political party
Bring judgment on sin	Because God is holy and hates sin	Because sinners are hassling me
Bring good weather	To help the farmers harvest their crops	So I can enjoy the beach

The possible examples are endless. The point is that prayers that sound alike on the surface can in reality be completely different in motivation. In some cases the motives are righteous. Yet when the motives are selfish and even sinful, God denies requests he may otherwise grant. The Word says, "When you ask, you do not receive, because you ask with wrong motives."

Selfish Pleasure Doesn't Work

One wrong motive deserves special attention. In a sense, it's the umbrella motive for all wrong motives: selfish pleasure.

Praying for selfish gain turns God against our requests. Tragically, selfish pleasure is the main reason many people pray. There are whole religious movements that teach this self-centeredness as the right way to pray—especially asking God for personal health and wealth. They say Christians are sick only because they don't ask God to make them healthy; Christians are less-than-rich only because they never claim the prosperity God has for them; Christians are unhappy only because they don't trust God to make them happy. The appeal is understandable, but "health and wealth" or "name it and claim it" teaching is contrary to the Bible. It borders on being cultic and sets up vulnerable people for great disappointment.

William Barclay, the famous British scholar, wrote that "the ultimate choice in life is between pleasing oneself and pleasing God." Lives set on selfishness and pleasure are basically unchristian. Luke 8:14 talks about the gospel of Jesus Christ as seed, explaining that "the seed that fell among thorns stands for those who hear, but as they go their way they are choked by life's worries, riches and pleasures, and they do not mature." It's easy to live for worries, riches and pleasures instead of living for God. I know from personal experience the constant tendency to want everything my own way. I can easily pray for God to make everything the way I want it to be, becoming consumed with myself and using God to accomplish what I want. With no trouble at all I can turn everything upside down and think of God as my servant to do what will make me happy instead of my being the servant to make God happy.

The night before the Battle of Tawara, World War II, fifteen soldiers met in a prayer circle with Chaplain Wyeth Willard. All fifteen, the chaplain reported, prayed pretty much the same prayer: "Lord, tomorrow we storm the beaches of Tawara. Our officers have told us this will be a bloody battle. Many of our number will be killed. If this has to be, Lord, let those of us who are Christians be killed. Spare those who don't yet believe so that they will have more time to make their decision for Christ. In Jesus' name. Amen." Those were prayers with high motives. They asked God not for their pleasure but for the good of others.

Those are motives that get God's attention.

Selfish prayers are rarely good prayers. When we are filled with ourselves our prayers tend to be wrong. When we are centered on Jesus Christ our prayers are likely to be right. Please don't misunderstand. It isn't that God doesn't desire our good. It isn't that God is stingy. It's that God wants us to pray with our hearts fixed on him, not on ourselves. Jesus explained that those who build their treasures on earth will experience corruption and decay. Those who seek God, God's kingdom and God's ways will get everything else they eventually need (Matthew 6:25–34).

One more important note before we leave James 4:3. In this verse there is an implied assumption that *prayers of request should never seek resources for personal pleasure.* Frankly, that disqualifies a lot of prayers. Think of it this way:

God will watch out for our pleasure.
We should primarily seek our pleasure in God as a Person, not in what he gives us.
We are part of a community of faith where Christians should pray for benefits and pleasures for *one another.*

God delights to give us good things, and he approves when we ask him to give us what we need. But prayer must first seek to please God and benefit others. Prayer isn't meant to be self-serving.

How Do I Know If My Motives Are Wrong?

Here's a sober truth: People with the worst motives are the ones who probably never bother to test their own motivation or to consider what God thinks. They pray for God's help to get even. Or for backs to step on as they climb the corporate mountain. Or even for skill to rob a bank, kill an enemy or seduce someone for sexual pleasure. Selfishness is blinding. It stops us from seeing reality, much less righteousness. With extreme selfishness comes extreme rationalization, concocting mental excuses that make the most sinful prayers appear legitimate and then blaming God for not granting what is requested.

For those whose hearts are hardened with selfishness there is only one solution. The supernatural conviction of the Holy Spirit brings a sinner profound awareness of his sinfulness. Awareness of sinfulness should lead a man or woman to repentance—a change of mind, a redirection of life. The person who experiences God's intervention will abandon selfish prayers and offer prayers for forgiveness. When God forgives sin and changes a heart, prayer will be motivated by love for others.

My immediate concern is for Christians with sensitive hearts who struggle to judge their own motives. They *want* to pray with right motives. They *try* to pray with right motives. But they continually worry that their personal sinfulness and inborn desires are getting in the way of their prayers and hindering God's answers.

Such a concern is often evidence itself that motives are right. Those who care enough to continually test their motivations are usually willing to submit their attitudes and desires to the Spirit's scrutiny. They don't have a problem with self-seeking prayers. But many still worry about it.

For those of a sensitive spirit, here are some practical suggestions for determining and eliminating wrong motives in prayer:

1. *Admit that your motives may be wrong.* This is an area of spiritual life where we are inclined to think ourselves better than we really are. Proverbs 16:2 candidly warns us that "all a man's ways seem innocent to him, but motives are weighed by the Lord." We want to look good. We give ourselves the benefit of the doubt. So we should begin by admitting the possibility/probability that our motives aren't as innocent as we may first judge.

2. *Ask God to search out and reveal to you any wrong motives.* This can be a painful prayer to pray. But when we realize that God's love and our benefit are the goal, the process is easier.

David gave specific advice to his son Solomon: "The LORD searches every heart and understands every motive behind the thoughts. If you seek him, he will be found by you; but if you forsake him, he will reject you forever" (1 Chronicles 28:9).

David spoke from experience. Years earlier he had taken Solomon's mother, Bathsheba, in an adulterous affair. At the time she was married to Uriah, one of David's closet and most loyal friends. Even after David committed adultery and murder, he wasn't clear about his own inner drives and sins. He prayed, "Search me, O God, and know my heart; test me and know my anxious thoughts. See if there is any offensive way in me, and lead me in the way everlasting" (Psalm 139:23–24).

3. *Ask the question: "Do I want to please God most of all?"* When critics questioned Paul's motives he offered a clear test in 1 Thessalonians 2:3–4. He said that his ministry and what he requests of God "does not spring from error or impure motives . . . On the contrary, we speak as men approved by God to be entrusted with the gospel. *We are not trying to please men but God, who tests our hearts.*"[2] Paul's practical test of his own heart was asking who he was trying to please. If he was trying to please God, his motives were good.

We can run the same test. When we wonder about what moves us to pray, we can ask, *Is this to please myself?* (wrong motive). *Is this to please others?* (wrong motive). *Is this to please God?* (right motive). The guarantee in this test is that God takes part. He tests our hearts. He knows who we aim to please. The trouble with this test is that it sounds as though our every prayer should be motivated with self-misery and self-sacrifice. This isn't true. Motives are rarely 100 percent pure. They are normally mixed, and nothing is wrong with our pleasure or with pleasing other people. The best motivation, however, puts God first, seeking God and his kingdom before anything or anyone else. It is giving God's pleasure majority consideration in every motivation and decision.

4. *Confess and clear out any sin or wrong motivation.* Once we acknowledge our sin or wrong motives we should confess them

to God, knowing that he will forgive every sin and remove any barrier. "If we confess our sins, he is faithful and just and will forgive us our sins and purify us from all unrighteousness" (1 John 1:9). The word "confess" means "to agree with." We should agree with God, in other words, that what we have done is sin and that our motives are wrong. Once we have done this, God agrees to forever forgive and cleanse away the wrong.

5. *Entrust your motives to God.* We don't have to look far in most churches to see that some Christians are perpetually introspective. They are convinced that their purest motives are somehow flawed. Regardless of what God and the Bible say they hold on to guilt that has long ago been forgiven. They seem to never see God's green light to move ahead. They never find freedom to serve God joyfully and pray to him unashamedly.

It may be that our greatest sin is failing to trust God to clarify our motives—along with a reluctance to embrace his forgiveness when we need it. It is an act of faith to believe that God will show us if our motives are wrong and forgive wrong motives so that they are no longer a barrier to our prayers. God calls us to follow these biblical steps and then to pray with a clear conscience and full confidence in God.

When our prayers have gone unanswered or been declined because of wrong motives, the place to begin is with God. To quit trying to use him and to start loving him. To ask him to take the center of life. To practice praying for what he wants, not what we want. We can ask him what we can do to make him happy instead of telling him what he can do to make us happy. There is a fascinating transformation that begins to take place when we do this. We discover in the God-centered life a level of satisfaction, contentment and pleasure that the fulfillment of all of our selfishness could never bring.

Prayer for Right Motives

Pure and perfect God, I'm struggling with my motives. I don't always know myself very well. Often I pray and really don't know whether my heart is good or bad. I need your help.

Search my heart. Reveal any wrong motives in me. Show me my sin and urge me toward full confession. Please, be gentle with me. Give me the courage to see myself as you see me.

I agree with you that I should not have done what I did. I agree with you that I should have done what I did not do. I agree with you that my motives have too often been to please me rather than to please you. I confess and ask for your forgiveness.

I accept your forgiveness. I believe you when you say that our relationship is right and our communication channels are clear. I feel good about you and that makes me feel good about everything else.

Now, Lord, I bring my requests with a full heart, with a desire to delight you, and with faith that you will hear and answer my prayers. Amen.

Notes

1. Emphasis added.
2. Emphasis added.

TEN

Does Prayer Change Things?

Millions of wall plaques declare, "Prayer Changes Things!" But is it true? Does prayer really make a difference? Many would be quick to say that "If prayer doesn't change things, then why bother to pray?" Isn't *change* the whole point of prayer?

Numerous scientific research projects are searching for objective proof that prayer can really change anything. Researchers at the University of Arkansas, for example, are analyzing the response of muscle cells to prayers from far away. Temple University researchers plan to use a research base of 150 high-risk infants for their determination of the effectiveness of prayer. Even the federally funded National Institutes of Health are sponsoring a University of New Mexico study to consider the comparative effects of Catholic, Protestant and Jewish prayers on patients with alcohol and drug addictions.[1] One reason for the sudden interest and funding is that Health Maintenance Organizations (HMOs) looking for ways to cut health-care costs want to know if prayer makes a difference.

The most famous test of prayer was conducted in 1982–1983 by Dr. Randolph Byrd, a California cardiologist. He recruited born again Christians to pray for 192 patients admitted to San Francisco General Hospital. There was a parallel control group of 201 patients not assigned for prayer. None of the medical staff knew which patients were getting prayer and which were not.[2] "Fewer patients in the prayer group required ventilatory support, antibiotics or diuretics," Byrd wrote in the 1988 *Southern Medical Journal*. "In the prayer group, 85 percent were considered to have a good hospital course after entry, versus 73 percent in the control group. . . . A bad hospital course was observed in 14 percent of the prayer group versus 22 percent of the controls." Byrd concluded that "intercessory prayer to the Judeo-Christian God has a beneficial therapeutic effect."[3]

Some discount such studies as unscientific, inconclusive or inappropriate. From a Christian point of view attempts at scientific proof of prayer's power introduce an inevitable problem. If they demonstrate that prayer indeed works in a scientific manner, then God has been reduced to a principle of physics. If they fail to show results from prayer, then God's supernatural power is discredited. The truth is that God is far more complex than our scientific methods can understand or explain.

Well, then, does prayer change things—or doesn't it? Before we try to answer this important question, think about what prayer is. Prayer is communion with God. Prayer is communication within relationship. From a biblical standpoint, *change* isn't primarily what prayer is all about. It is more about love and relationship with God.

Imagine a man and woman who agree to date. While at a party in his apartment the woman sees a plaque on the wall that says, "Marriage Changes Things." She laughs at first, but then discovers he's serious about it. When she asks him what the plaque means, he says, "There are a lot of things in my life that I don't like and I want changed. I drink too much. I'm deeply in debt. I don't have a job. All of my former girlfriends are mad at me. I want to get married so all of those things can be changed. I want to get married so that I can have what I want and be happy."

Amazed at his ideas, she asks, "What if marriage won't change the things you want changed?"

He replies, "Why would I bother to get married if marriage didn't change the things I want changed?"

If this woman is smart she will bolt from the apartment and never date him again. As attractive as her boyfriend may seem to her, she wants a husband who marries her because he loves her, because he wants to be with her—because of their *relationship*. She doesn't want to marry a man whose reason for marrying is to get his life changed around—even though some or all of those changes might actually come about with marriage.

God has feelings, too! He welcomes prayer. But prayer to God is about love and relationship and communication, not about making God into a celestial genie in a prayer bottle who will grant our wishes when we ask. It's true that changes do come from a personal relationship with God and that prayer is an important means to change. But that is secondary to what prayer is essentially about. Prayer would be a glorious and wonderful privilege even if nothing changed, just because prayer is our means of connecting with God. Prayer is primarily about *God*, not primarily about *change*. It's against this backdrop of understanding prayer that the main question of whether prayer changes things is broken down into four parts: *Does prayer change God? Does prayer change circumstances? Does prayer change others?* and, *Does prayer change me?* Let's look at these questions separately.

Does Prayer Change God?

Recall the story of King Hezekiah, who was diagnosed to die and yet understandably pleaded to God for life. God had said Hezekiah would die. Yet, after he prayed, God said, "I will add fifteen years to your life" (2 Kings 20:6). Prayer changed God.

But theologians object to the idea that prayer can redirect God, saying that God cannot change. God is immutable. God is unchanging. God himself declares, "I the LORD do not change!" (Malachi 3:6). Hebrews 13:8 teaches that "Jesus Christ is the same yesterday and today and forever." If God can and does change, nothing and no one in the universe is constant. And if there is nothing constant, there are no absolutes. Everything leads to chaos.

Here we cross a line into the mysteries of God that we will never fully understand. Some explain that God chose the change before we asked; he knew we would ask and knew his answer would be yes. Others think God chooses to leave some options open—dependent on whether or not we ask. Still others recognize that the person praying may have done the changing to fit what God already decided.

Part of the mystery may be appearances. What to us looks like divine change is really an unfolding of God's plan. We see only bits and pieces of the unfolding drama. Like a mountain road with hairpin curves and switchbacks, God's plans may look as though they are changing back and forth when they are really rising as planned to God's predetermined conclusion.

The truth is that we don't know exactly *how* this seeming change works. We don't know because God never told us. Either we would not have understood or God didn't want us to know. We do know that it *does* work. People pray and God acts in ways that look to us a lot like change. Hezekiah probably didn't try to trace intricate theological arguments. As far as he was concerned he prayed and God changed the prognosis. That was good enough for him.

Does Prayer Change Circumstances?

Therefore confess your sins to each other and pray for each other so that you may be healed. The prayer of a righteous man is powerful and effective.

Elijah was a man just like us. He prayed earnestly that it would not rain, and it did not rain on the land for three and a half years.

Again he prayed, and the heavens gave rain, and the earth produced its crops.

James 5:16–18

Does prayer change circumstances? The clear teaching of James 5:16–18 is that the prayers of righteous persons are powerful and effective. Elijah prayed and circumstances changed.

Anyone who has lived in farm country has prayed many times for God to change the weather. In the spring and fall the prayer may be for clear skies and drying winds so the field can be plowed, planted or harvested. If the fields are too wet for tractors the crop may be planted too late to mature fully. Or it could rot in the fields if it isn't harvested on time. During the growing season, in contrast, no rain means no growth. Drought can be disastrous.

Elijah prayed for drought and no rain fell for three and a half years. He prayed for the drought to end and the rains returned.

"Mere coincidence!" the skeptic insists. Perhaps, although Christians will insist that there are a lot of coincidences when they pray!

Circumstances reflect God's answers to our prayers. They are God's way of speaking his care and closeness to us.

God communicates and relates in different ways to different persons, especially people from different cultures. Language is the most obvious example. Since I don't read or understand Swahili, Japanese or Portuguese, God doesn't communicate with me in those languages. My experiences with God are in the English I speak and understand. I read an English Bible. I pray in English. I praise and worship God in English.

However, just as God uses different languages to relate to his people, he also uses different ways of communicating beyond language. These include *dreams, visions* and *circumstances.*

The New International Version has 210 references to dreams or visions. Ancient people expected God to speak to them through dreams, visions and similar experiences. An angel of the Lord spoke to Joseph in a dream (Matthew 1:20) and told him to take Mary home as his wife, even though she was pregnant. Zechariah saw a vision in the Jerusalem temple (Luke 1:13–20) telling him that his wife would bear a son (John the Baptist) and that he would lose his power of speech until the time of the birth. Just as ancient people experienced God through dreams and visions, many modern Christians still do. Some are in the United States, though most are in other countries and cultures.

More common among North American churches is for us to experience God through the circumstances around us. It is common to hear believers say, "The Lord was so close to me. He spoke to me through everything that happened that day." We are more likely to pray for God to alter the circumstances of our lives than ask him to speak to us through a vision. When we pray we expect God to change circumstances more than we expect God or an angel to appear in a dream.

I look for God in circumstances. I believe that he is the Lord of everything and that by his power and providence he fulfills his purposes in the billions of circumstances that occur every day. That doesn't mean that every circumstance is God-given or God-pleasing. Certainly evil is fulfilled through circumstances as well.

Yet a world where God never intervenes in response to our requests is hopeless. If God doesn't change circumstances, then prayer becomes absurd. Worse yet, if God doesn't change circumstances, then his very power and presence also become unbelievable and untrustworthy. Believing that God is both powerful and present means that I acknowledge him to work through circumstances. If not, I am forced to say that God is powerful but too distant to become involved in our world and my life, or that he is involved but too weak to make a difference.

That makes it most appropriate for me to talk to God about my circumstances and to expect to experience God through what happens. Nothing is too big. Nothing is too small. God can change circumstances for finding a parking place or for stopping the deployment of a nuclear bomb.

Does Prayer Change Others?

Some of our most impassioned prayers are intercessory prayers—prayers for someone else. Parents praying for children. Prayers for husbands or wives. Prayers for churches and companies and countries. Every day there are billions of prayers to change someone else.

The Bible has many examples of prayers for others. It also has many commands to pray for others:

> Love your enemies and pray for those who persecute you. . . .
>
> Matthew 5:44

> Pray that I [Paul] may be rescued from the unbelievers in Judea and that my service in Jerusalem may be acceptable to the saints there.
>
> Romans 15:31

> And pray in the Spirit on all occasions with all kinds of prayers and requests. With this in mind, be alert and always keep on praying for all the saints.
>
> Ephesians 6:18

> I [Paul] urge, then, first of all, that requests, prayers, intercession and thanksgiving be made for everyone—for kings and all those in authority, that we may live peaceful and quiet lives in all godliness and holiness.
>
> 1 Timothy 2:1–2

God calls us to prayer for others on the assumption that prayer will make a difference. God will effect change. That is the purpose of intercession.

We must be careful, however, to guard against any notion that our prayers can overrule either the will or sins of another person. God allows people to make bad choices and to sin. If another person chooses to commit murder, to be immoral, to abuse or otherwise to do what is wrong we cannot force them by our prayers to do what is right. They make their own choices. Those choices may be terrible. They may harm others. We can and should pray for God to influence others through circumstances and conscience so that they do what is right. But he leaves each of us to choose for ourselves.

After the death of his father a teenage son became estranged from his family. Stephen rebelled against his mother's care and ignored his younger siblings. Moving out on his own, he chased a life of drugs, immorality and the occult. His mother wept. She pleaded with God for her son to return to God and his family. In his late twenties the son repented. The pain he had experienced made him an effective witness to teens and families in crisis. God used many tools to prod the son back to faith, including the Bible, a powerful conviction of sin and the straight-talking words of his younger sister. Did his mother's prayers effect change in Stephen? Yes, of course. Did he decide for himself? Yes, he did.

Perhaps the most painful part of praying for others is the lack of guarantees. It's possible for another mother to pray just as long and hard without her son ever responding as Stephen did. The responsibility to pray is God-given. God expects us to exercise that privilege. He will answer those prayers by acting with a powerful influence against sin and toward righteousness in the other person's life. Yet God will also allow that person to choose—and to sin.

Does Prayer Change Me?

The fourth and final question is usually the one we ask least: "Does prayer change me?" In practical terms it's the most important question of all.

Jesus believed that the answer to this question is an unqualified *yes!* On that night before he was crucified he prayed profusely for himself. When he took a break from his prayers and talked to his three best friends he told them likewise to pray for themselves—"so that you will not fall into temptation" (Matthew 26:41). Jesus knew that life is a spiritual battlefield. Every Christian is threatened by mines in the ground and bullets in the air. Temptation puts us all at risk that we might be blown apart by sin. Praying for ourselves is the best protection. The prayers themselves aren't what protect us. They are the means of deploying the great forces of God in our lives.

Prayer's first goal isn't to change God's mind to do things *my* way. It is to change me to do things *God's* way. It's like taking a car in for a wheel alignment. All the driving, turning, bumps and potholes throw the wheels out of line with the car's frame. The technicians don't bend the frame to match the wheels. They adjust the wheels to line up with the frame.

The same is true for me. Every day I need to be realigned with God: my thoughts with his thoughts; my will with his will; my life with his life. Yes, prayer changes me.

Praying for Real Change

Before we leave the question "Does prayer change things?" consider a few added notes:

1. *In your prayers, center on Christ, not on change.* Change without Christ is worthless. Christ without change is impossible. Seek Christ more than change in order to get the best of both.

2. *Prayer is relational, not mechanical.* Why is it that when elders pray for the sick to be healed sometimes it works and sometimes it doesn't? Because all of prayer is woven into the complexities of relationship. It's not a mechanical transaction like pushing a button.

I only have to push an elevator button once to get the elevator car to come and the doors to open for me. People aren't like that. Saying "Come!" to a husband or to a wife is seldom a good approach. Relationships include time, intimacy, reconciliation and much more.

Don't ever think of prayer as a way of pushing God's button and demanding immediate results. Remember that prayer to God is always connected to relationship with God.

3. *God delights to give us good.* When we pray we can be encouraged by remembering who we are talking to. God is our loving Father. He's always on our side, delighting to do us good and give us good.

When Jesus taught on prayer he told us to ask. He let us know what to expect. He compared our prayers to a child's asking a human father for food. "Dad, please pass the fish." What father would give his son a plate of poisonous snakes? Or if a son said, "I'd like an egg," what father would put a scorpion on his plate? Jesus drew this comparison: "If you then, though you are evil, know how to give good gifts to your children, how much more will your Father in heaven give the Holy Spirit to those who ask him!" (Luke 11:13).

God the Father is better than the best of human fathers. He doesn't trick us. He won't harm us. He never seeks to give us evil. He is a wonderful father who delights to give us good.

Two Different Answers

Theressa Frost received two different answers to two sets of ·prayers for physical change:

> The signs had been there for years. All the pain, the infections, the positive tests were ever-looming evidence of the pyelonephritis and the resulting kidney damage. Surgery done in 1951, after the birth of my third child, had corrected the drainage problem from the right kidney but didn't stop the aggressive infections. The birth of an additional child in 1955—after receiving advice to have

no more—damaged the kidney even more.

So now it was pay-up time. I was nine months into my college degree program when I relented to the pain long enough to see a kidney specialist. After studying the X-rays his first comment was, "If this were my kidney, I would get rid of it as soon as possible." I was almost in shock, never dreaming of his suggesting such a thing. Another surgery, more medication, certainly—but not losing a kidney.

I had been told not a month before that I needed a hysterectomy because of prolonged, profuse bleeding, and now this. How could I cope, much less stay in college to see my long awaited dream of obtaining a degree become reality? My frustration and emotions were suddenly overwhelming. Could God tell me *no*?

After much confusion, fear, emotions and prayer, I decided to call my pastor and request that the elders of the church pray for me. That very evening he and about ten of the elders came to my home and prayed with me and my husband. One elder had great hope for my healing and believed it would happen. I never believed I would be healed, but I did think I was doing what God wanted me to do according to Scripture.

Time went on with much reluctance on my part to take action. But the pain and illness brought me up short, and I decided to schedule surgery to remove my right kidney the day before Thanksgiving. My family supported what I decided and rallied around me to encourage and love me. Surely God was saying *no* to healing.

The kidney was removed, followed by an extremely slow recovery. The doctors never promised a thing, since it was impossible to tell if my left kidney would take over the job. They couldn't know how fast my body would compensate for the overload of healing and throwing off the poisons of illness. Healing came slowly, not miraculously as I had asked God to do. It was God's healing power that won over, but in the way he planned and not the way I asked. I never had to have the hysterectomy.

That problem slowly resolved itself. The kidney grew to take on the burden for the whole body. I will always be on antibiotics and always subject to extreme infections that take over once in a while, but God gives grace and strength.

The second time I called for the elders to pray for me began quite innocently. My husband and I attended a junior high chicken barbecue at church. The meal was delicious, but as I took a last bite of chicken I felt a small, sharp bone in my mouth. I involuntarily swallowed it. Troubled breathing and increasing misery led me to the hospital emergency room where extensive exploration showed no bone. But there were problems with my esophagus. It could have been damaged by the bone or maybe by the examination. They kept me overnight in the hospital.

During the night I developed some serious, erratic heart rhythms, which caused them to relocate me to the Cardiac Intensive Care Unit. A series of specialists came to examine me—none of whom could find the cause for my intense pain and increased swelling. Finally the team of physicians decided that the cause was a punctured esophagus, which had caused mediastinitus—an inflammation like peritonitis, except in the chest space behind the sternum. I had one collapsed lung and developed double pneumonia. Doctors installed chest drains and a feeding tube.

Twenty days later my esophagus still hadn't healed. My pastor and his wife visited and I asked when it would be a good time for the elders to pray for me. He said "Anytime!" That evening the elders came to the hospital and, with my husband and son, joined hands around my bed praying for me. I truly believed Christ was there laying his hands on me, healing me in body and spirit. I told them that I believed all God was asking me to do was to be obedient, and that I had fulfilled that by asking the elders to pray for me. I was immensely grateful.

After they left, the nurses came in to work on me and

had a series of problems with uncontrolled drainage from wounds and fouled IV lines. Then the problems all came under control. The next day the specialist checked the drains and noted the vastly improved appearance of each one. I did another dye test to see if the esophagus was healed, and there was significant improvement. Later I had an X-ray taken that showed complete healing of the esophagus. I was able to eat again for the first time in a long time. The specialist had been talking about further surgery and the need to send me home with a feeding tube and liquid food. But God spared me all that. God had healed me and I praised him, then and now. This time he said *yes!*

Does prayer make a difference? Absolutely! . . . but not always as we ask. For Theressa Frost the first answer was *no* and the second *yes*. Both times she trusted God and both times God gave clear answers to specific prayers.

Praying About Change

Unchanging God, change me!

I admire your consistency. I am grateful for the truth that you are always the same. I am amazed that you can be the same and not be boring. You are always exciting. There is so much to you. You have infinitely more facets than any diamond. You appear more beautiful in every light. You are the stability of the world and the strength of my life.

Lord, I want to be like you. Oh no, I don't want to be you. I'm not asking to be God. I just want your likeness to be seen in me. Change me—chasing out every sin, filling me with your good. Help me to see everything from your point of view. Reshape me to desire what you desire. Make me a tool to accomplish your purposes.

If I wait until every needed change is made in my life before I pray for others, no intercessory prayers will ever be heard from my lips. So I must pray now for your mercy and grace in the lives of my family, the people of our church, the leaders in authority, the poor and needy, the sick and hurting, the spiritually lost and rebellious and all others that your Spirit brings to my mind and tongue.

Without full understanding of how you effect change, I give to you everyone and everything that needs changing. I shall keep on praying whether I see those prayers fulfilled in my lifetime or not. I will trust you to do your great good in the lives of those I know and love . . . convinced that you know them far better than I, believing that you love my beloved more than I could ever love.

In the name of the Christ who makes my transformation possible. Amen.

Notes

1. Joseph Pereira, "The Healing Power of Prayer Is Tested by Science," *The Wall Street Journal* (Wednesday, December 20, 1995), p. B1.
2. Ibid., p. B8.
3. Eric Zorn, "Let Us Pray," *Notre Dame Magazine* (Autumn 1995), p. 48.

ELEVEN

Asking Again and Again

"My story of unanswered prayer has to do with our adopted chemically dependent daughter" is how this praying mother begins.

"We have been on our knees in prayer for her for thirteen years. She began using alcohol and drugs when she was fifteen years old, unknown to us. We have never seen her drink or use drugs in all those years. She started running away from home at the age of fifteen. She got into trouble with the law. She has been in very dangerous and very negative surroundings. She has been a victim of domestic abuse.

"We have reared her eight-year-old daughter since she was three years old—as our daughter's addiction progressed she wasn't able or willing to help her. It is sad and so painful. We continue to pray every day and we're trusting God for the answers. We have tried everything. We have been in every support group possible. We need wisdom and guidance in rearing our grandchild. We need prayer support. We hear from our daughter two or three times a year at the most."

Is it time for this couple to give up? Should they quit praying? There is a special story from Jesus for this couple and all other Christians who have prayed for a long time without receiving the deep desires of their hearts.

Jesus' Story for Those Tempted to Give Up on Prayer

> Then Jesus told his disciples a parable to show them that they should always pray and not give up.
>
> He said: "In a certain town there was a judge who neither feared God nor cared about men. And there was a widow in that town who kept coming to him with the plea, 'Grant me justice against my adversary.'
>
> "For some time he refused. But finally he said to himself, 'Even though I don't fear God or care about men, yet because this widow keeps bothering me, I will see that she gets justice, so that she won't eventually wear me out with her coming!'
>
> And the Lord said, "Listen to what the unjust judge says. And will not God bring about justice for his chosen ones, who cry out to him day and night? Will he keep putting them off? I tell you, he will see that they get justice, and quickly. However, when the Son of Man comes, will he find faith on the earth?"
>
> Luke 18:1–8

This is one of the strangest and most encouraging parables Jesus told. Unlike some of Jesus' parables, this one begins with the point Jesus is making. It's his story for those who are tempted to give up on prayer, those who have prayed and not received. It's for those who are weary and discouraged in their praying. It's for those of us who have considered all the possible explanations for unanswered prayer and don't know what to do next. Jesus gave this story to all of us to show that we "should always pray and not give up."

It's a story especially for those who agonize over the inequities of our world. Where is God when gunmen open fire on innocent victims in shopping malls and post offices? Why does God allow mothers and fathers to inflict such harm upon young children? What about the honest student who receives a lower grade because she refuses to cheat on a test? Consider the godly single mother who prays for her former husband to send the child-support check she and her child desperately need but never receive. Sometimes we want to scream with outrage. "Where is God?" we want to know. "Where is justice?"

We think about taking the situation into our own hands—hiring a lawyer, buying a gun, making a scene in public or anything else that might make a difference. In many situations we *do* need to take action—though in a godly way. But the first and continuing response of Christians to every forbidding situation is that we "should always pray and not give up."

The Characters: A Judge and a Widow

The first-century judge in the story wasn't Jewish. Within Jewish culture, cases such as this were taken not to the civil courts but to the elders of the synagogue, who heard the dispute between the principals in the case and made a decision. From that Jewish tradition we get the New Testament instruction that Christians not sue one another in the secular courts but ask the church to arbitrate their differences (1 Corinthians 6).

Even when first-century Jews used civil courts there wouldn't have been a lone judge making the decision. Ancient laws required three judges, one chosen by each party plus an independent judge who joined the case as the tiebreaker.

All of this information tells us that the court official in Jesus' story must have been a Roman judge. Notoriously corrupt and unjust, Roman judges based their decisions more on bribes than on law or evidence. Everyone knew that if the plaintiff didn't have enough money to pay off the judge—or refused to pay off the judge—the case could not be won.

As if general reputation and corrupt practices weren't enough, this particular judge "neither feared God nor cared about men." He was an especially bad person in an already unjust legal system. He cared only about himself. He didn't determine the cases before him on the basis of testimony or law. Hurt or suffering people didn't bother him at all. He was a man without conscience, a man without religious faith. Think of him as tough, selfish, unfair, arbitrary—and powerful.

He wasn't the first or last of his breed. We live in a sinful world where bad people rise to power and where good people become subject to their sinful whims. Nazi prison camps were filled with soldiers like this. Ugandan dictator Idi Amin empowered wicked men to carry out terrible acts in the name of the government. Terrorists around the world past and present manipulate or defy the law to fit their own politics and cause unspeakable suffering to ordinary people. But there are also such people in the management of our companies, the offices of our government, the chambers of our courts and the rooms of our homes. They can and do make life miserable for those who do right and walk in integrity.

In the city of this oppressive judge lived a woman who was the victim of injustice. Widowhood is seldom easy. But it was especially difficult in ancient times, where there was no life insurance, no survivor's benefits or modern means for a widow to support herself. Many widows were exploited, made to lose what little they did have. In response to this problem both the Old Testament and the New Testament call on God's people to protect and provide for widows.

Since Jesus didn't tell us this widow's particular plight, we can only guess. Perhaps some powerful landowner confiscated her property. Maybe she was denied a rightful inheritance from her husband's estate. Perhaps one of her children was illegally sold into slavery to pay for her debts. Apparently she was poor, powerless and desperate. If the judge didn't help her no one else would or could. Persistence was the only tactic she had left. She pleaded with the judge to "Grant me justice against my adversary."

The judge refused. He didn't care about her. So what if she was oppressed and desperate? He didn't think it was his problem. He refused and wrote her off.

She asked again.

He refused again.

She asked again.

He refused again.

She kept asking. He kept refusing.

We can picture her waiting outside his court, following him down the street, approaching him in the marketplace, nagging him all the way home. Day after day she refused to take *no* for an answer. She was desperate and desperate people don't easily give up. There is no luxury of pride or embarrassment or politeness. She begged and pleaded and persisted and petitioned.

She wore down the judge! He made an interesting, exasperated response: "Even though I don't fear God or care about men, yet because this widow keeps bothering me, I will see that she gets justice, so that she won't eventually wear me out with her coming!" This widow was an amazing person. She wore down—perhaps intimidated—this tough, compassionless Roman judge. He didn't change his character, get religious or enjoy a touch of pity. He admitted that he still didn't have time for God or compassion. He still didn't care what other people thought about his actions. He gave the widow what she wanted just to shut her up. She was the widow who wouldn't quit taking on the judge who didn't care.

The Contrast: The Judge and God

Many of Jesus' stories draw a comparison that says God is *like* the person in the parable. This time Jesus made a contrast instead.

God is not like the judge! That is Jesus' sharp contrast. Jesus asks two rhetorical questions and each has an obvious answer:

Will not God bring about justice for his chosen ones, who cry out to him day and night? The obvious answer is *yes!* God will bring justice to Christians who pray to him the way the widow pleaded with the Roman judge.

Will he keep putting them off? The obvious answer is *no!* God won't keep putting off the persistent prayers of Christians who keep on asking him the way the widow kept on asking the Roman judge.

The judge was unjust.	God is just.
The judge lacked compassion.	God is compassionate.
The judge didn't care about people.	God cares deeply about people.
The judge was in no hurry.	God is speedy.

Understand what this means to us. When we face injustices, God cares. When we are the victims of discrimination because of race or age or gender, when we are wronged for doing right, when the courts fail to render a fair verdict, when sinners win and saints lose, when we are desperate like the widow, God will listen with compassion and act with speed. When all of our other alternatives are exhausted and we are absolutely desperate, when we go pleading to God in prayer, God isn't like the judge. God listens. God cares. God acts.

But . . . "That's a wonderful, wonderful teaching from the Bible," you say. "Such sweet words are encouraging to hear. But it just doesn't ring true. My own experience is just the opposite. I lost a promotion because I refused my boss's sexual advances. I did what was right and he did what was wrong. I tried everything to be the perfect employee and nothing ever worked. Now I'm right where I was four years ago. He's become vice-president of the company. I've asked God thousands of times to make this right and it stays wrong. I have the impression that God either doesn't care or is powerless to act. He's anything but speedy. I want to believe what the Bible says, but I have to tell you that I think God is a lot more like the unjust judge than Jesus says!"

These are hard statements to answer. Yet I believe what Jesus says: "God brings about justice for his chosen ones." How do we reconcile the Bible's declaration with our personal experience?

God doesn't see things as we see them. He sees time as a whole. We see time in bits and pieces. Compare it to seeing a man with a knife cut open another person's chest and slice out that person's heart. If that was all you saw you would feel pity for the victim and anger toward the assailant. But if you were to see more—the time before and after—you would realize that the victim is really a patient and the assailant is really a surgeon. Without cutting there could be no transplanting. Without present pain there could be no future years of life. Furthermore, the conversations after the surgery amaze you with contradictory perceptions. For the patient and family the procedure was extraordinarily long, while the surgical team delights in how quickly and well everything went.

So it is with God. He sees the whole picture. Time is not to him as it is to us. What we think is too many years, he knows to be speedy indeed. What we reckon as needless and disastrous, God sees as necessary and purposeful.

Understand the height of God's commitment to righteousness and justice. He is the standard of justice. He is the maker of righteousness. He is irrevocably and eternally committed to making things right. *And he will do it!* In his right time he will punish sin, right wrongs, vindicate those who have been the victims of unjust judges and inequitable circumstances. God is far more committed to making things right than we ever could be.

For us the pressing question isn't whether God will hear our prayers and make everything right. The question is this: Will we keep praying? God won't quit on us, but will we quit on God? That's why Jesus asked whether "when the Son of Man comes, will he find faith on the earth?" Jesus was wondering if anyone would still be praying and believing when he returns to earth to answer our prayers and make all thing right.

What to Do? What God Will Do!

Mothers seem to be the last to give up praying. The widow in his story was probably a mother, and maybe if Jesus were telling the story in modern America his illustration would be of a single divorced mother like the fifty-seven-year-old woman who was afraid to keep asking others to pray for her problem son. Her prayers for her children began in 1972, when she became a Christian. She was already a single mom with two children. She began to pray for their salvation, for their safety, for their future life partners and for God's good in their lives. "We worshiped in a small Bible-teaching church and had many families that supported us emotionally and were our friends. During those years I prayed for a Christian man who would come forward and give some time and emotional support to my son as a role model, but no one ever cared to do that.

"In 1972 my son was seven years old. Even before the divorce he had shown signs of being 'hyper,' or what today would be termed ADD. We worked with psychologists and the school system and the pastor to help control his behavior. Nothing seemed to work.

"I went to work with a Christian youth organization and we prayed every week for him and for me to be the right kind of Christian mother. He spent time at a Christian camp but wasn't taken with it. His release-time teacher was someone I knew, and she prayed for him every week.

"His behavior deteriorated over the years and although he

went through several short-term treatments and one six-month treatment ordered by the court, he never was straight. He was kicked out of the army for drugs. He has spent time in jail and has just now been released from a year in prison, not for anything serious but for an old offense for which he never completed his probation requirements. While locked up he has been ministered to by prison ministries, but when he comes out he goes back to his old life.

"To make a long story short, today he is thirty-three years old. He is living in Texas where he has lived for the past ten years. Maybe the fact that he is alive is some answer to all these prayers for him. But his life is lived on the edge of the gutter—not exactly a street person, but he has times when he has been homeless. I'm grateful that he isn't a criminal and that he and I have a good relationship over the phone.

"People don't ask me about him much anymore, because it's the same old story. Even his father, who married again and isn't a believer, gave up on him totally about three years ago, as a lost cause. My own family only asks infrequently how he is doing.

"There are many times when I feel God hasn't heard all these prayers and I hesitate now to ask for prayer again and again in new groups—because I never can come back to these sincere pray-ers with anything but the same old story. I know there are faithful people like his release-time teacher and my close friends who still pray for him.

"When I hear the success stories of changed lives, I wonder if I will ever see his life changed."

This mother's story triggers understanding from some of us, identification by a few of us and compassion from all of us. It is so difficult to love so much, pray so long and keep on hoping when there seems to be no basis for hope.

There are some prayers we can let go of with relative ease. We can get over lost opportunities, small dreams, hopes for a life that goes a little easier.

There are other prayers where circumstances force us to let

go. God's *no* is permanent and obvious. The disease didn't go away. The son flunked the course. The battle was lost.

But there are other prayers we cannot—*should not*—stop praying. Prayers for friends who find life a constant physical or psychological or spiritual struggle. For rulers and people in authority. For our own and others' spiritual maturity. For loved ones and the lost wherever they are who still don't know Christ. To give up on these prayers denies the deepest longings of our hearts, our sense of what is right and good, and our faith in God's power and presence. Until God says *no* in a clear and unmistakable way *we are to pray.*

That's the point of the parable. To keep on praying. Jesus is saying, "Don't quit. Don't give up."

Perseverance is hard for us. We belong to a culture and a generation where patience is unusual. We want everything immediately. Impatience causes us to give up on marriages that might be reconciled, become hopelessly discouraged with problem children before God is finished with them, and quit jobs when something goes wrong rather than persevere and see the good God plans to do.

Not everyone easily quits. Some persevere through extraordinary adversity. They are like the widow in Jesus' story.

God wants us to keep on praying. Keep on asking. Jesus is saying, "Don't be discouraged. Don't assume that God doesn't care. Don't think that the answer will never come. Don't accept injustice as inevitable."

Listen to Jesus when he encourages us to "always pray and not give up." He promises that God will answer. The God who made the world, holds it in his hand and someday will bring his plan to completion, will make wrong into right and bad into good, working everything together for his glory and our benefit.

There is only one way you will buy into all of this. You've got to have faith. You must believe that Jesus knew what he was talking about. You have to believe that God is all he claims to be. You must accept God's promises even if they seem to contradict your experiences. What do you think? What do you say? How do you answer Jesus' question, "When the Son of Man comes, will he find faith on the earth?" Say, "Yes! I believe. I won't quit. Jesus will find faith in me. I'll keep on praying!"

My Persistent Prayer

God, I'm going to ask you again. You've heard this same prayer many times before. I've asked it every way I can imagine. Every time you've said no or nothing at all. But I'm back with the same request. And I'm not going to give up. If it takes ten thousand times or more, I'll ask and ask and ask.

My persistence isn't from a lack of faith. It is the deepest expression of my faith in you.

I believe you are God.

I believe you can do anything.

I believe you hear every prayer I pray.

I believe that you want the very best for me.

I believe that you will someday answer yes.

But those are not the biggest reasons I keep asking. I ask again and again because Jesus told me to. He said that I should not give up, so I won't.

Until you clearly tell me to quit, I'm going to ask you every day.

I'm excited about you and what you soon will do.

In Jesus' name. Amen.

TWELVE

Responding to Rejection

The same sun melts the wax and hardens the clay.
—Ancient Greek Proverb

A young seminary student was working part time in a local church. One of his first assignments was hospital visitation. The church secretary gave him a pack of file cards with names and basic information about parishioners he was to visit in several urban hospitals.

On the seventh floor of the first hospital he entered the room of a woman in her fifties. He introduced himself as a pastoral intern from her church, but she interrupted before he could finish. "It's about time you showed up!" she said. "Look, I'm packed and ready to leave here. And I'll be glad to be done, because this is a terrible place. The doctors hardly ever come around. The nurses are rude. The food is terrible. I'm going to protest my bill when it comes. I can't wait for my family to pick me up—if they ever show up. Can you believe that they hardly visited me during my week in this awful place?"

The young pastor-to-be tried to spark a conversation, but she listened little and complained more. She aimed her anger and bitterness at God, the hospital, the church and the young man in her room she had never before met. When he finally escaped he was exhausted, relieved to be away from her.

In the hall he read the next card with his next assignment. It was another woman of similar age—same floor, same hospital. He felt like skipping her and going home. He didn't feel up to another emotional beating. But he forced himself to walk down the long hall and into the room of another person he had never before met. There were hints along the way: a sign that said *Oncology*, patients who had lost their hair, families gathered in vigil around hospital beds. He had entered the cancer ward. And when he saw the woman whose name was on the card he quickly concluded that she had come to the hospital to die.

Once again he introduced himself as a pastoral caller from her home church. She immediately smiled and said, "Now, young man, you didn't have to come to see me. There are plenty of other folks who need your visits far more than I do." He was drawn to her warmth and love. She asked him about himself and made him feel important. She was genuinely interested. When he asked her about her experience on that floor of the hospital she was delighted to talk. "This is a wonderful hospital!" she explained. "The doctors make extra visits to see me. The nurses are so competent and so kind. The food is just wonderful. And I've had so many visitors that I've lost count."

I don't know if the first woman had prayed for God's healing. I'm not even sure she was really sick, at least physically. It does seem that she was bitter and ungrateful.

Certainly the second woman must have prayed. She knew she was going to die, and that prompts us all to prayer for healing and life. But God had told her *no*. She hadn't become bitter. She didn't resent the answer nobody wants. Somehow she trusted God and claimed his grace. She knew the God of hope.

How We Respond

When Christian author Larry Burkett spoke publicly about his battle with cancer, he acknowledged the reality of an uncertain future. Convinced of God's unwavering love and care, he said, "Don't ask God 'Why?' He probably isn't going to tell you anyway. Ask God 'What do you want me to do now?' "

How we respond to the divine *no* is just as important as our prayers. It can be the difference between bitterness and victory.

To be frank, we cannot overrule God. When he gives his answer we cannot appeal to some higher power. He *is* the highest power. We *can* keep praying. We can plead. We can cry. We can ask others to pray. All of those may be very appropriate actions. But when the *no* is *NO!* there is only one choice left for us—how to respond.

We may accept God's answer with the perspective of Job, who was plagued with misery and misfortune:

> Naked I came from my mother's womb,
> and naked I will depart.
> The Lord gave and the Lord has taken away;
> may the name of the Lord be praised.
>
> Job 1:21

These words are amazing—especially in view of the man's misery when he spoke them. Even more amazing is the biographical addition that "In all this, Job did not sin by charging God with wrongdoing" (Job 1:22). There is no pretense that Job liked God's answer, but he refused to hate God. He accepted and respected God's right to do whatever he chose to do with him.

That is in sharp contrast to those who responded to a plague: "They cursed God on account of the plague of hail, because the plague was so terrible" (Revelation 16:21).

I have heard and seen men and women turn bitter because of unanswered prayers. Their disappointments have included infertility, unemployment, illness, bankruptcy and death. I have

seen others who have become equally resentful over slight of-
fenses, trivial misfortunes and hurt pride.

And I have watched in awe as Christians have buried the
children they prayed to be healed, lost companies they asked
God to bless, faced rejection they did not deserve—all with
"love, joy, peace, patience, kindness, goodness, faithfulness,
gentleness and self-control" (Galatians 5:22–23).

I can draw only one conclusion from these observations.
How people see life on the far side of unanswered prayer isn't
really determined by what outward ill they suffer when God
refuses their request. How they handle God's *no* is decided by
their individual, inward response. Some turn *against* God for
not getting their way. Others turn *toward* God with a conviction that God loves them no matter what happens.

Because I haven't suffered all the problems of others, because I haven't walked in their shoes, because I haven't prayed
their prayers and been turned down, I cannot guarantee how
I would respond. It certainly isn't my place to judge how others
handle their hurts. But I know how I want to respond. I want
to believe God has every right to give any answer he chooses.
I want to maintain the conviction that God's love isn't to be
judged by my personal circumstances. I want to wholeheartedly love God and enthusiastically trust God no matter what.

There are some simple steps of response to God's *no* that
we do best to learn ahead of time. It's much more difficult to
master these lessons of response in the heat of disappointment.
There are three:

Lesson One: Seek an Explanation

When God says *no* it is good for us to ask *why*. Go back to
the reasons God may have said *no* and see which applies:
  1. Are my prayers not in my own best interest?
  2. Are my prayers contradictory?
  3. Are my prayers inappropriate?

4. Do I have a wrong relationship with God or someone else?

5. Does God will something different?

6. Is the time not right?

7. Is something else more important?

8. Do I pray out of wrong motives or with wrong reasons?

Ask God to tell you why he turned down your prayer request. Ask for the Holy Spirit's wisdom as you carefully weigh each possibility. Take your time. Wait for God's answer.

This may not be an easy process. It takes prayerful biblical thinking, a heart open to God and willing self-examination.

And this process usually requires the help of other Christians. Biblical Christianity is lived in community. Since we are often blind to our own faults and need the perspective of others, the explanation for unanswered prayers often comes from other believers. Identify the Christians around you who have demonstrated gifts of wisdom, knowledge, faith, discernment and encouragement (1 Corinthians 12), and seek their counsel on why you have prayed and heard *no* or no answer at all.

Within the Christian community we are told to "Confess your sins to each other and pray for each other so that you may be healed. The prayer of a righteous man is powerful and effective" (James 5:16). It's interesting how often Christians quote the last part of James 5:16—the claim that our prayers are powerful and effective. Yet seldom do we include the first part of the verse—the exhortation to confess our sins to each other in the church. The body process of discerning the cause of unanswered prayers is the neglected prerequisite to praying prayers that are powerful and effective.

In 1 Thessalonians 5:11, Christians are advised to "encourage one another and build each other up, just as in fact you are doing." Usually we think of this as a responsibility to comfort others. That's good to do. But the verse also implies a benefit for us. We will receive encouragement from other Christians. This is of vital importance when we struggle with life's issues and are unclear why God doesn't heed our prayers.

We can turn to fellow Christians for emotional and spiritual support and for the direction we need in seeking the reason our prayers aren't working.

Unfortunately, I need to insert a word of caution. Some Christians are self-appointed personal prophets who spew damaging counsel. One such man went to the home of a terminal cancer patient and asked him to name the sin for which God was judging him. He told the dying man that if he would confess that sin he would be healed of his malignancy. Needless to say, the visitor was presumptuous and inappropriate. On another occasion a couple went to visit the parents of a desperately ill baby and told them the reason their baby didn't get well was because they didn't have enough faith. "If you really believed God," they said, "your prayers would be answered and your baby would live." This isn't just poor theology. It's spiritual cruelty. This couple assumed that God kills babies because their parents fall a few inches short of faith. That isn't the loving and grace-filled God of the Bible.

Those who make promises *for* God can undermine the faith of those who feel betrayed by those unfulfilled promises. That's what happened to a professional writer who prefers to remain anonymous:

> Thirty years ago, at nine years of age, I was diagnosed with a disease that millions of people live with—diabetes. The injections, the diet and the awful urine tests—it was all overwhelming for a child. So when my parents, my pastors and every Christian leader I knew told me that I could be healed, those were the very words I longed to hear. If I would just have faith, they told me, and meet a few simple conditions (being prayed for by the elders, confessing my faults to one another), I would be healed. If I would only keep my part of the bargain, God could certainly be trusted to keep his part. My eager little spirit clung to this belief wholeheartedly. What a wonderful God! He had good plans for me; this is how he would demonstrate his love.

Over the years I prayed constantly for healing and was prayed for often by ministers and church elders. My faith was deep and sincere. I truly loved God and felt that I was seeking the Giver, not just his gifts. But I wanted this one particular gift more than anything and I devoted all of my energies to qualifying for it. I refused to entertain the mere suggestion of doubts—after all, that might negate all of the faith I had cultivated, everything I had worked so hard for.

After seventeen years, though, I could no longer ignore the possibility, however heartbreaking, that God's answer might be *no*. Almost as soon as I had accepted that, the whole structure of my faith crumbled. Having been influenced at an impressionable age to believe I would be healed, my very concept of God had been built around his promises to heal. That was who he *was* according to his own Word. If God could not be trusted to be true to his Word, how could he be trusted at all? I didn't know what to believe. I felt hurt, rejected, betrayed and confused. In the end, it wasn't the injections and diet that were difficult to live with, but the feeling that God didn't love me.

For two years I didn't consider myself to be a Christian, even though I had graduated from Bible school. But slowly, gradually the Holy Spirit began the process of drawing me back to faith. Little by little I began to understand who God is and how he interacts with us. When God didn't do what I expected, I had questioned his character, not my expectations. I had questioned his Word, not my interpretation of it. It was painful to abandon my dreams, but I had to let go of my conception of what God ought to do and how He ought to show his love. I had to let him be Lord of my life and accept his answers.

I still don't have the answers to life's great questions; I don't expect to in this life. But I believe that when we reach heaven, all our questions will vanish with just one glimpse of Jesus. They simply won't matter anymore in the light of his presence. As P. T. Forsyth said, "We shall come one day to a heaven where we shall gratefully know that God's great refusals were sometimes the true answers to our truest prayers."

As a postscript, I believe that Christians should be careful of encouraging others to believe that God will perform miracles in their lives. God does many things that we don't understand; we must be honest about that and avoid the inappropriate application of his Word to others' lives. In our zeal to build their faith, we could destroy it.

How do we get the wisdom of the best counselors and avoid the devastation of the worst? The answer is simple to explain—but difficult to accomplish in a crisis. Healthy churches give ample opportunity to exercise spiritual gifts and demonstrate spirituality. When a person proves through the months and years that he has been gifted by God with an ability to wisely discern spiritual matters, that person can be trusted in a crisis. If the counselor is self-appointed and self-righteous, the advice is rarely worth hearing.

Back to the list of eight reasons God says *no*. If some of those explanations obviously don't apply, eliminate them from the list and concentrate on those that are most likely. Ask God if they are the explanations you seek. Then use them to change your prayer, change your behavior, change your relationships, or accept God's answer as a final *no*.

Often God will make his answer clear. Remember that God is our loving, kind and generous heavenly Father who delights to give us good gifts. When we ask him for an explanation he often explains. He wants us to know. God isn't playing a hide-and-seek game with us. God desires our prayers and desires to answer our prayers.

If no answer to the *why?* questions comes, God may be telling us that he's not going to tell us. That's what happened to Job. Sometimes God won't tell us. As hard as it can be, we need to accept that.

When our children were young they sometimes asked for things they wanted and were told *no*. Then they asked why.

Sometimes Charleen and I had to say, "We're sorry, but we just can't tell you. You'll have to accept *no* for our answer without knowing the reason why." Sometimes we had already gotten what our child wanted. It was hidden in a closet or under a bed or at a friend's house waiting for Christmas or a birthday. Sometimes parents say *no* for good reasons that just shouldn't be explained.

Lesson Two: Submit to God's Decision

Whether or not God explains, our next action is to submit to his decision. That's what trust is all about.

Once we know that God has declined our request, submission requires acceptance of God's choice. Faith requires confidence in God's decision.

Marty has repeatedly asked God to provide the $10,000 she needs to send her disabled son to a special school. Every prayer seems to receive either a *no* or no answer at all. She has asked God why he won't supply the needed money. She has prayerfully considered possible answers to her question. For a long time she pondered her motives and decided they are pure—she truly has her son's best interests at heart. She knows of nothing contradictory or inappropriate about her prayer. She has reviewed her relationships with God and others, confessing every known sin to God, even going to a neighbor she once offended to make that relationship right. While it's possible the time may not be right, it seems to her that it might be too late to help her son if he doesn't attend the special school this year.

She admits that God might have something more important in mind, though she doesn't know what. It could be that God wills something different, yet she can't identify why or what. Realizing that she may be spiritually blinded by her strong desire for the money and schooling, Marty asked three godly Christians from her church to pray with her. These two women and one man listened as she shared the whole situation.

They reviewed with her all the possible explanations for God's *no*. Marty made it clear that she really wanted spiritual discernment; she wasn't using this as a backdoor method to get their money for tuition. They prayed with her and for her.

In other words, Marty did everything she knew to do. The money still didn't come. Finally she prayed, "God, all I know that is left to do is assume you don't want us to have the money and that you don't want Kevin to attend Thompson Heights School. I honestly don't understand. I don't know why. But if that is your desire, I submit to it. In fact, I pray that your will be done, not mine. If you don't want Kevin in the school, I pray that he will have no way to attend that school." That was one of the hardest prayers Marty had ever prayed. But she meant it. True, she was greatly disappointed, but she gained a peace of heart and contentment that God's will is best and her submission was the right thing to do. She agreed with God that she would no longer seek ways to get the money—no more requests to friends, loan applications at the bank or plans to hold garage sales.

Submission sends a clear signal to heaven that we acknowledge the Lord's supremacy. We admit that we aren't God. We acknowledge that we aren't smarter or better than God. We refuse to pretend that we could do God's job better than he can.

Lesson Three: Repeat Requests

The third response to God's *no* is to ask again. But doesn't that contradict everything in my last point? Isn't presenting another request to God the opposite of submission? What about trust? Once we have fully submitted to the Lord, shouldn't we just give up and accept *no* for God's final answer?

Jesus didn't accept *no*. Paul asked repeatedly when he was turned down. In a relationship of mutual love and trust, there is no contradiction in accepting God's *no* and yet asking him again and again. Neither Jesus nor Paul were out of line. Neither sinned. Neither offended God by the intensity or repetition of their prayers.

I have requests that have been on my daily prayer list for years. Some I have prayed thousands of times. I've sought explanations. I've submitted to God's decision. Yet I am convinced that God hasn't released me from asking again. Even though I am ignorant to the reasons, I am convinced that these are prayers God wants to hear. It may be to keep me humble. It may be to convince me that he will answer even though my wait will be long. It may be that I will never know why.

While there is nothing wrong with repeated prayers, we just need to be sure that they are preceded by an effort to understand, paired with a responsiveness that removes the barriers God reveals to us and a self-examination that ensures we have truly submitted our wills to God.

Distinguish Between Self and the Request

When we respond to God's *no* it's important to distinguish between his rejection of our request and his acceptance of us as his children. God's acceptance of a person as his child is permanent. Christians are adopted (Ephesians 1:5) into the family of God. Even though God hates sin, God loves every one of us to the extent that not even our sins cause God to reject us as persons. The love of God is infinite, the grace of God beyond human comprehension. God always has our best interests in mind.

Sometimes it is grasping God's love for us that best helps us come to peace with God's rejection of our prayer requests. He cares too much to grant anything that would harm us.

When we pray urgently for God to grant our requests it can be hard for us to distinguish between who we are and what we want. When God says *no* we may feel an intuitive sense of personal rejection. We can harbor the hurt until we distance ourselves from God. We might become like pouting children who don't get their way. More often, we feel deserted by God and don't want to face the One who has rejected us.

As difficult as it may be to implement this advice, we must subject those bruised feelings of rejection to the truth of God's love. It's when we have been turned down that we should quickly return to God in prayer to share our feelings and receive his healing love.

A Case Study: When You Are Sick

Sickness triggers more fervent prayers than anything else. Sickness renders us needy—often desperate. Everyone experiences the simple sicknesses that make us uncomfortable. Some of us know the severe sicknesses that cause tremendous pain and threaten to steal life itself away. Whether you are the patient yourself or someone you know and love is ill our humanity is never more vulnerable than when sickness strikes.

God's healing is an absolute wonder. Few experiences cause faith to be strengthened and soar like healing from God. We love him more, trust him fully and thank him from the depths of our hearts.

When a healing doesn't come, it can be faith-threatening. Those who pray for relief from pain that only gets worse, those who plead for the life of a child who dies, those who are convinced God will say *yes*, and he says *no*—all of these begin to wonder if God exists, or what kind of cruel God he must be if he does exist.

All of our hurts and hopes, fears and faith, plus a thousand questions bubble to the surface with the New Testament words in James 5:14–15:

> Is any one of you sick? He should call the elders of the church to pray over him and anoint him with oil in the name of the LORD. And the prayer offered in faith will make the sick person well; the LORD will raise him up. If

he has sinned, he will be forgiven.

These words of James are written to Christians. Obviously Christians become sick just like everyone else. That fact is the expectation of the Bible and the experience of all Christians. The popular misbelief that Christians are exempt from disease and never subject to sickness isn't taught in the Bible. It is contrary to orthodox Christian doctrine. It is inconsistent with experience. Christians are different not in the troubles we face but in the responses we live out.

1. *Sick Christians should ask for prayer.* Recognizing that Christians do become ill, James 5:14 says that sick Christians should ask for prayer. James offers no description of how sick a person must be before calling for prayer, making that decision a matter of personal judgment. Routinely praying for one another in simple sicknesses or during the early signs of disease seems most appropriate, but these verses seem to imply more serious illness. Calling the elders of the church to pray over a runny nose or muscle cramp seems inappropriate.

A key point is *who* takes the initiative—it is the sick person. It isn't the responsibility of the church or elders to know who is sick and run out to offer prayer. It's the responsibility of the Christian to call for help. This may be a passing technicality when a person is well, but it's an important point to remember when you become ill. Take the initiative. Be responsible. Call the church when you are going into the hospital!

2. *Help comes from within the church.* The elders pray and anoint. The church mobilizes to help Christians who face personal needs.

This assumes that every Christian is already part of the church before sickness or another crisis arises. Sadly, there are needy Christians who aren't connected. They face crises ranging from unemployment to divorce to sickness or family death with no church to come alongside them. They ask for prayer from a congregation and no one knows who they are.

Being connected when illness or other tragedies strike us

is one of many reasons every Christian should have a church home—why we should make an effort during life's calmer moments to join, get involved and build relationships. The New Testament assumes that we live as part of an interdependent Christian community—when others need help we help them, and when we need help they help us. That includes calling for the elders to pray and anoint when we face illness.

3. *The elders rally to pray for healing—in faith.* Elders are the spiritual leaders of the church. They aren't just those who hold official titles or positions in a church. In some situations the needs may be far greater than a handful of leaders can handle. The church can share the responsibility among men and women recognized for their spiritual leadership even if they don't currently hold official positions.

When a request comes forth, the elders are to gather with the sick person and pray *in faith* for healing. That doesn't mean they have faith in their prayers. It doesn't mean that they have faith in healing. And it doesn't mean they have faith in faith. It means they have faith in God. The elders are to pray with absolute confidence that God hears, God cares and God has the power to heal. If that faith is missing they fail as elders and their prayers are worthless. The prayer should be sincere, strong and compassionate, passionately desiring healing, fully confident in God.

The elders—when requested—may anoint the sick person with oil in the name of the Lord.

Oil may have a medicinal purpose. In the first century, olive oil and similar oils were widely used as medicine. The Good Samaritan, for example, poured oil into the wounds of the man who was assaulted and left to die by the roadside (Luke 10:34).

James 5:14, then, could be given the modern translation of "pray over him and give him penicillin in the name of the Lord." Christians should take full advantage of the benefits of physicians and modern medicine—although making sure that medical help is preceded and permeated with prayer and that the medicine is taken "in the name of the Lord." Physicians treat the sickness, but it is God who heals.

The oil may have a religious purpose. It seems better to understand the oil as a symbol of God's presence and power—just like anointing a person to be a king, just like laying hands on a person as a symbol of God's touch.

When we are sick we often need something more than words to help us experience God. The oil is a physical reminder of the invisible Lord.

The form of the anointing isn't described. It may have been poured on the head or on the part of the body that was afflicted. In many churches today, it is usually a simple smearing of olive oil on the forehead of the person requesting the anointing.

More important than the oil is "the name of the Lord." It is the formal recognition that Jesus Christ makes the difference. The elders pray and anoint representing the patient to the Lord and the Lord to the patient. It may not make too much difference if the oil is omitted, but it makes a huge difference if Jesus Christ is omitted.

4. *Christians embrace God's promise of wellness.* "Does it work?" is the question we all want answered when we study the teachings of James 5:14–15. The Bible seems clear and direct: "The prayer offered in faith *will* make the sick person well; the Lord *will* raise him up."[1] Is this an absolute guarantee—or are there some implied conditions?

Apparently it doesn't work every time. If it did, there would be few Christians in hospitals, Christians would have no need for health insurance, and there would be few if any dead Christians. There must be millions of Christians over the past two thousand years who called the elders, were prayed over and anointed, and yet didn't receive the healing they asked for. Because Christians do not believe the Bible could lie, we conclude the promise must be conditional.

Some say the condition is *adequate faith.* When healing doesn't happen, it is either because the sick person or the prayer team didn't believe hard enough. Shortage of faith produces continued sickness. This idea can be brutal. I have heard accusations that children have died because parents or elders didn't exercise enough faith. It makes God out to be exceedingly cruel. He is portrayed as a God who allows innocent children to die because some adult's faith rated only 2.3 on a faith scale when God needs at least 2.5 to perform a miracle. While faith is important, *faith doesn't heal.* God heals—and God has a record for doing great things in response to minimal, mustard-seed-size faith.

The real reason some are healed and some are not is that God chooses it to be so or not. We would like to wrestle free of this conclusion, to lay blame at the feet of anyone but God. But true faith believes that the ultimate and best choice is made by God and not us. We usually don't know how God decides; we believe that whatever he decides is right. That is faith in God.

5. *The Lord heals and forgives.* The key point is *who* does the healing. "The prayer offered in faith will make the sick person well; *the Lord will raise him up.*"[2] God is the Great Physician. God is the one who raises up the sick. The power is his. The decision is his. The healing is his. The credit is his. God may give healing that is complete and permanent, or the healing may be partial and temporary. The healing may be direct—without a physician or medicine involved—or the healing may be indirect, using whatever means God chooses. The healing may be immediate—at the moment of the prayer, or the healing may be gradual or suddenly come later.

And it is the Lord who forgives. "If [the sick person] has sinned, he will be forgiven." Just as we all get sick, we all sin. We need to have our sins forgiven, and only God can do that. It is more important to be healed spiritually from sin than physically from sickness.

Sometimes the two are connected. Some people are sick because of their sin. In order to get well physically they need to be forgiven and healed spiritually. God can do both. That isn't to say that all sickness is directly caused by a person's sin.

Nor is it to say that those who aren't healed are holding on to their sin. The Bible gives examples of people who were sick because of sin. And the Bible gives examples of sickness that was not caused by sin. The point is that God and only God has ultimate power over all the physical and spiritual needs of our lives.

What would I do with all of this information if tomorrow I were diagnosed with a terminal illness? It's difficult to predict our future responses. I know what the Bible says. I know what I should do and what I hope I would do. It's my wish list for holding fast to God during hard times:

I would immediately pray.

I would ask God to give to me his care, his perspective on my illness and his will for my life or death.

I would probably pray for healing—the sooner the better, as easily as possible, by whatever means God chooses.

I would utilize every resource God has given me, including the best of medical treatment and the prayers and the support of fellow Christians in the church.

I would specifically ask the elders of my church to come to my home, pray for me and anoint me with oil in the name of the Father, the Son and the Spirit.

I would ask God to explain *why* if my prayers were not answered, asking especially for him to show me if there is anything wrong with me or my prayers that I can change to make a difference.

I would repeat my prayers often.

I would ask others to keep on praying for me.

I would commit to give God the glory regardless of the outcome.

I would agree that God knows best and submit my will to his will.

Prayer for Healing

My Father and Lord, I pray to you in the name that is above every name—the name of Jesus Christ.

I pray in obedience to the instructions of your Bible. I pray with faith in you—I am absolutely convinced that you will hear, that you have the power to heal and perform miracles, and that you are a God of infinite love and compassion.

You know the needs and the hopes of every person. You know about the pain, the tumor, the injury, the disability, the stress, the disease, the fear. You know what medicine can do and you know what you will do.

In the name of Jesus Christ, please heal. Raise up those who are down low. Relieve pain. Restore health. Cure disease. Forgive sin.

Hear my prayers. Hear the prayers of your church. Hear the prayers of the elders. Hear the prayers of these who come to you for help and healing. Hear our prayers and answer with your powerful touch.

God, I not only believe you can heal but that you will heal. I promise not to take credit for myself. I won't say healing happened because of my prayers, a human touch or the anointing oil. I will say what I know to be true—that it is you and you alone who will raise up and that to you and to you alone belongs all the credit and glory.

Heal your disciples. In Jesus' name. Amen.

Prayer for Prayers Rejected

Listen, Lord! Please, listen! I come in the name of Jesus Christ to ask you my most important question. Why?

Why have you said no?

Is it because of something I have done wrong? If so, please show me my sin and I will confess it and I know you will forgive me. Forgive my selfishness, my pride, my contradictions, my misdirected motives.

Is it because of a wrong relationship? Show me whom I have offended. Direct me to those with whom my relationship isn't right. Teach me all I should do to make amends, to reconnect, to heal and to love. Give me the grace to be at peace with all persons.

Or was it you, Lord? How have I offended you? Are you hurt by my lack of interest in you? Is it because I have so often crowded you out of my life? What have I done wrong that I must confess? What should I have done that I did not do? More than anyone else, I want everything between you and me to be right. Please, my Lord and Friend, reconcile us to each other.

Are you telling me to wait? Then, with the help of your patience, I will wait until your right time has come. Until then, shall I keep praying over and over what you have laid on my heart to ask?

Do we will the opposite, God? Is it that what I want isn't what you want, and what you want isn't what I want? I submit my will to your will. I will accept whatever you say is right and good. Because I believe in you, I also believe in whatever you choose. Not my will but yours, my Father.

And if there is no answer, I will accept your message of silence. In some ways, that would be the hardest of all, but it isn't my place to make you speak or to tell you what to say. If your answer is silence, I will trust even that answer is from you. Amen.

Notes

1. Emphasis added.
2. Emphasis added.

THIRTEEN

When No Becomes Forever

Janet and Duane Willis left Chicago in November 1994 on a trip that would take the lives of six of their children. Before departing, Duane bowed his head in prayer "asking that God would protect us and give us a great trip, a good time together and, of course, safety." While driving along the Interstate highway toward Milwaukee their Plymouth Voyager minivan ran over a piece of metal that had fallen from a truck ahead of them. The metal flew up and punctured the gas tank, causing the minivan to burst into flames and explode.

The Willises were able to exit the front doors as five of their children were consumed by the flames. The oldest was eleven, the youngest six weeks old. Thirteen-year-old Ben was severely burned.

Standing next to their charred car and the bodies of their children, Duane turned to Janet and said, "This is what God has prepared us for." As they rode behind the ambulance transporting their children's bodies Janet quoted from Psalm 34

(KJV), which had been memorized by the congregation of Parkwood Baptist Church, where Duane is pastor: "I will bless the Lord at all times. His praise shall continually be in my mouth." Verse 19 says, "Many are the afflictions of the righteous."

From their own hospital beds they prayed for their son Ben to live. He died the next morning.[1]

Where do we turn when the time for praying has past? What do we do when the person we love has died, when our wife or husband has left and married another, when the prodigal child has said a permanent goodbye? What is left when God's *no* becomes forever?

There is a hollowness of soul that seems to take up permanent residence where once hope lived. It is hard to go on, much less trust God or even talk to him. There is a harsh meaning to the cruel but common expression "this is past praying for."

The wife of an executive was recently praying for a friend to come to faith in Jesus Christ. A month earlier he had been diagnosed with throat cancer. Her prayers were abruptly ended when he jumped off the roof of his New York City condominium to his death. What should she now say to God?

Lynn Vandergriff, a Minnesota homemaker says this: "My mother was a Christian Scientist. That's how I was raised. When I became a Christian as an adult, I sought to share my faith with my mom. With a thousand miles between us, she in New Jersey and I in Iowa, it wasn't easy. I began to pray that God would prepare my mom so that on my next trip home we could talk easily about salvation. It didn't go well. Perhaps it was because I was too new in my own understanding or maybe just because I was her daughter. I continued to uphold her in prayer. When I found out she had cancer I took my request to the church. This time I prayed God would allow someone to witness where I could not. I brought up the subject on my last trip home. She turned away and made no comment. Pain? Fear? I don't know.

"She took a sudden turn for the worse and died within the week. As far as I know she died without accepting Christ. I didn't understand why and felt maybe I had said or done something wrong. Months later I walked out in tears during a sermon on hell, not wanting to believe God would have allowed Mom to go there. I cling to the hope that maybe she did acknowledge Christ as her Savior, but I will never know for sure until I get to heaven."

The pain is powerful in the story of a pharmacist named Mary, who gave birth to a baby girl named Jill in May 1991. Born two months early, Jill was oxygen deprived during birth and died in her mother's arms when she was only one day old. "This broke my heart as well as my husband's," says Mary. "As we grieved Jill's death we also knew we wanted another baby as soon as possible. In trying to conceive again we ran into unexpected infertility problems and had a miscarriage right before Christmas—I was three months pregnant. We continued to pray for a baby—obsessively we prayed. Our two-year-old, Ida, always asked Jesus for three babies—one for herself, one for Mommy and one for Daddy. We conceived again only to miscarry again. More people began to pray for us. We conceived again, but miscarried again also. After three miscarriages we went to a specialist.

"After four months we conceived. We prayed every day that this pregnancy would be a healthy one. Many, many people prayed with us. When we were two months along we discovered that we were expecting triplets. We immediately found out that a triplet pregnancy is very high-risk—the risk being pre-term birth resulting in possible birth defects or death. We decided to take all precautions and to pray continually. We got on the prayer chain at almost a dozen churches and I spent most of my pregnancy on complete bed rest. Every day we prayed as a family for our babies. We thought surely we had paid our 'dues' and that we would be 'successful' this time.

"We discovered at five months that we were having two girls and one boy (just what Ida had asked for—a girl for herself, a girl for mommy and a boy for daddy). We named them Anna Elise (after my mom—this was Ida's baby), Emily Elizabeth and Ethan Alexander.

"The pregnancy continued fine and I was able to give birth eight months into the pregnancy. Several hours after the birth we received the horrifying news that Anna had a severe congenital heart defect. She had surgery scheduled for her fourth day of life. Again we contacted everyone to pray. We prayed. While she survived the surgery she died in my arms when she was just seven days old. We wanted to die too. Telling Ida was pure hell. My heart was completely broken. I felt so abandoned and alone, so forsaken and so deeply saddened. My faith was completely shaken.

"Late one night I was feeding Ethan and Emily. I was exhausted and found myself praying: 'Jesus please help me. I'm so tired. Please help my babies to eat and to sleep.' When I discovered myself praying I got angry, very angry—and thought to myself, 'That's it! I'm not praying for my children anymore. God doesn't listen! He has allowed two of them to die plus the three miscarriages. Maybe I didn't pray for Jill all that much during my pregnancy with her, but I did pray. But with Anna I prayed for several years for her conception, prayed constantly during my pregnancy and pleaded with many others who committed themselves to pray as well. And God said *no*. He let her die! I can't trust my children to him anymore. He doesn't care. If he knits them together in the womb—well then he's dropping a few stitches because they aren't coming out healthy.'[2] I was very sad. I was very scared for my faith and for my four-year-old's innocent faith. Her first big prayer in life, and God lets 'her baby' die.

"I have sought pastoral counsel, am trying my best to model a living faith to my children, and I have recently joined a Bible study. I have tried to pursue my faith and wait for my feelings of closeness to, and love from, God to return to my life. It is now four and a half years since Jill's death and two years since Anna's death, and it still seems like God has moved to Mars. I'm trying to be a patient waiter but I really miss feeling that God loves me and cares for me and my children. Accepting his *no* and his love is difficult."

There are no adequate words of comfort when hope is lost, dreams are shattered, lives are lost and God's *no* has become permanent. Those of us who have not traveled someone else's path must be exceedingly careful we don't offer pat answers and easy solutions. The pain is real. We do not fully understand and God has kept many of the answers we want to himself.

Perhaps the counsel of Pastor Duane Willis carries extra power because he knows the awful sights and sounds of his children dying and the finality of God's *no*. He says that "God knows all of history and times from its beginning to end. What happened to us wasn't an accident. God is never taken by surprise. God had a purpose for it, probably many purposes. We don't understand God's agenda—as Isaiah says, 'His ways are not our ways.' We asked him for safety and it didn't turn out that way, but it's in the way God answers our prayers that we come to understand what God's will is."[3]

It finally comes down to trust. When all the prayers have been prayed and all the answers have been received, we must decide if we will believe that God is good even if we weep over the answers he has sent. To put our trust in the Lord isn't just counting on him to give us what we want but believing that he loves us and has cared for us even in the wake of tragedy. It's the conviction that God knows best and that in heaven we will be able to ask him to explain what doesn't make sense to us here on earth. It's the deep belief that God has an explanation that is good and right.

Some missionaries labored for years trying to find a word for "trust" in the new language they were deciphering and recording for the first time. One day their native helper plopped down in exhaustion in a hammock, using a word that meant he was "putting all his weight on" that hammock. It was the word the missionaries decided to use for "trust" when they translated the Bible into that language.

To trust God is to put all of our weight on him. When we don't understand, when we hurt, when we suffer disappointment, when we are past asking for something or someone, when we feel furious over the outcome—then trusting God is finally just collapsing in exhaustion on him. That is when prayer comes back to its purest meaning of *communion*. When we are on the other side of asking we simply come to God for who he is and connect with him in the most basic expression of faith.

Years ago I heard the story of an awful tragedy. A driver's school bus stalled on railroad tracks when a train was coming. He unsuccessfully tried to start the bus and then got as many children out as he could before the train ripped through the vehicle and its small riders. There was an enormous loss of life including the driver and his own children. The bereaved parents and people of the community took out their hurt and anger on the driver's widow. She not only had to deal with the loss of her husband and children but with the blame that somehow was being transferred to her.

When a friend many miles away heard what had happened he sent a simple but profound telegram: *Remember—God is too wise to ever make a mistake and too kind to ever do anything cruel.* I believe the telegram told the truth. But it implies a necessary response. It is a call back to the kind of faith that puts all of our weight on God, convinced that his love is greater than any of our experiences that may tempt us to doubt him.

Wise and good God, sometimes it isn't easy to say, "I trust you." What I wanted so much you did not give. When I was so sure you would say yes you said no. When I still had hope it ended forever.

Can you feel my pain? Do you understand what I am trying to say to you? Are you still listening to me? Will you hear and answer this prayer?

I have run out of words to say. Let my heart speak to your heart. As best I can I will trust you. Give me more faith. I will put all my weight on you. I will believe you for everything I cannot know. I will interpret life by who you are and not by what happens. I will trust you to give me new hope and greater faith.

If I lose all else, I will have you. And you are all I really need. Thank you, Jesus. Amen.

Notes

1. Eric Zorn, "Let Us Pray," *Notre Dame Magazine* (Autumn 1995), pp. 44–45.
2. Reference to Psalm 139:13: "For you created my inmost being; you knit me together in my mother's womb."
3. Zorn, loc. cit.